Anonymous

Register of Confederate Soldiers who Died in Camp Douglas, 1862-65 and Lie Buried in Oakwoods Cemetery, Chicago

Anonymous

Register of Confederate Soldiers who Died in Camp Douglas, 1862-65 and Lie Buried in Oakwoods Cemetery, Chicago

ISBN/EAN: 9783337307295

Printed in Europe, USA, Canada, Australia, Japan

Cover: Foto ©Suzi / pixelio.de

More available books at **www.hansebooks.com**

REGISTER

—— OF ——

ONFEDERATE • SOLDIERS

—— WHO DIED IN ——

CAMP DOUGLAS

· · · · · 1862-65 · · · · ·

—— AND LIE BURIED IN ——

OAKWOODS CEMETERY

CHICAGO, ILLS.

1892

COHEN & CO., CINCINNATI.

✶ OFFICERS ✶

OF THE

EX-CONFEDERATE ASSOCIATION OF CHICAGO.

Incorporated March 29, 1890, Office of the Secretary of State, Illinois.

"CAMP NO. 8, UNITED CONFEDERATE VETERANS."

BY GENERAL ORDERS No. 8,

FROM H. Q. U. C. V., ATLANTA, GA., MAY 13, 1891.

PRESIDENT, JNO. W. WHITE.
1ST VICE-PRESIDENT, R. H. STEWART.
2D VICE-PRESIDENT, GEO. FORRESTER.
SECRETARY, R. LEE FRANCE.   TREASURER, SAM'L J. SULLIVAN.
ASS'T SEC'Y, JERE S. WHITE.   HISTORIAN, JNO. G. RYAN.
SERGEANTS-AT-ARMS—CHAS. R. TUCKER, T. F. LINDE, W. B. PHIPPS.

CONFEDERATE DEAD.

The graves of the Confederate dead buried at Oakwoods Cemetery are, by governmental authority, placed under the control of the said Ex-Confederate Association; and that body has, by enactment, authorized and empowered Comrade Jno. C. Underwood to raise funds for the purpose of erecting a monument in honor of their memory, and with which to take proper care of the special burial grounds assigned to its charge; and the said Jno. C. Underwood, having been appointed and commissioned Major-General to command the Division of the "United Confederate Veterans" in the Northern States west of the line of the Alleghenies, is charged with the care of

— 3 —

the Confederate dead buried at or near the sites of the prison camps Morton, Chase, Douglas in Oakwoods Cemetery at Chicago, Johnson's Island, Cairo, and other places within his Division District.

See transcript of official documents as follows:

THE EX-CONFEDERATE ASSOCIATION OF CHICAGO,
"CHICAGO CAMP No. 8, UNITED CONFEDERATE VETERANS,"
CHICAGO, June 26, 1891.

Resolved, That Comrade Jno. C. Underwood be appointed a committee of one, with power to take any necessary action, to raise funds for the purpose of building a monument over the 6,000 Confederate dead in Oakwoods Cemetery, Chicago.   [Signed]   JNO. W. WHITE, *President.*

ATTEST:

[Signed]   R. LEE FRANCE, *Scretary.*

HEADQUARTERS UNITED CONFEDERATE VETERANS,
NEW ORLEANS, LA., Nov. 21, 1891.
GENERAL ORDERS No. 22.

I. In order to properly and faithfully carry out the "Benevolent and Historical" objects of this organization, as has been requested, the General commanding deems it necessary to form two divisions in the Northern States, one east and one west of the line of the Alleghenies, each to be officered by a Major-General, who will be appointed by him upon the recommendation of the Confederate Veteran Camps in Chicago, Ill., and in New York City, to be made not later than December 15, 1891.

II. It will be the duty of these Major Generals when appointed to organize camps and take steps to care for and assist the disabled, indigent, helpless and distressed ex-Confederate soldiers and sailors in their respective departments, and to protect their widows and orphans; also to have charge of the Confederate dead buried at Gettysburg, Fort Warren, Camps Morton, Chase, Douglas, Oakwoods Cemetery at Chicago, Johnson's Island, Cairo and all other points; to care for and have the graves of the known and unknown dead annually decorated, to preserve and protect the headstones; also to obtain and compile the names and commands of all the Confederate dead buried at every point in the North, which lists this Association will publish through the medium of its camps all over the South, so as to give relatives and friends correct information of the last resting places of these Southern heroes, their and our beloved dead, thus rescuing their names from oblivion and handing them down in history.

In this philanthropic and holy work the General commanding, and these headquarters will render all possible aid.

By order of   J. B. GORDON, *General Commanding.*
GEO. MOORMAN, *Adjutant-General and Chief of Staff.*

HEADQUARTERS UNITED CONFEDERATE VETERANS,
NEW ORLEANS, LA., Dec. 19, 1891.
GENERAL ORDERS No. 26.

I. The General commanding, heartily approves the recommendation of the Ex-Confederate Association, Chicago Camp No. 8, and Jno. C. Underwood, of Chicago, is hereby appointed Major-General of the division in the Northern States west of the line of that Alleghenies, to date from December 7, 1891.

II. Major-General Jno. C. Underwood will carry out the provisions of General Orders No. 22 from these headquarters, and his attention is especially directed to the " Benevolent and Historical " features of it.

III. The General commanding, hereby approves the action of the Convention of Delegates assembled at Ocala, Fla., on the 16th inst., in compliance with General Orders No. 24 from these headquarters, in the selection of J. J. Dickinson for Major-General of the Florida Division.

IV. Major-General J. J. Dickinson will immediately enter upon the duties of the office, and will be obeyed and respected accordingly. His attention is directed to Article 10 of the Constitution, and he is urged to hasten the formation of new camps in his division.

By order of J. B. GORDON, *General Commanding.*

GEO. MOORMAN, *Adjutant-General and Chief of Staff.*

APPEAL FOR MONUMENTAL AID.

To Former Comrades in Arms, Sympathizing Citizens of Southern States, and to Whomsoever Else it may Concern :

FRIENDS—There are over 6,000 Confederate dead buried at Oakwoods Cemetery, in the city of Chicago, Ills., of which number more than 4,300 have been registered by name, company, regiment and State ; the remainder, owing to the destruction of the registers at the time of the great fire in 1871, cannot be traced further except in numbers, thereby making the probable aggregate as roundly stated above.

Under authority from the proper officers of the general government, it is the intent of the " Ex-Confederate Association " of Chicago to erect a suitable and appropriate monument over such soldier remains and otherwise care for the graves and special burial grounds within the cemetery previously named, and with that view the undersigned has been selected to raise the necessary funds for successfully carrying out the purpose.

Therefore, he appeals to all sympathizers, without regard to their locality or condition, to contribute such a sum as each can afford to bestow for the worthy purpose.

To die at any time is the hardest service a soldier can render to his people, but to die in a prison hospital far from family and friends and be buried beneath soil away from home and in a then adverse section, is the giving of life for the " lost cause," under such circumstances, as might well awaken sympathy even among the most unimpressionable. The soldiers of the Confederacy who died within the borders of Southern States have not been forgotten, and their graves are kept green and constantly cared for by loving hands; is it then not a noble charity from all, and a sectional duty from comrades and Southern people

— 5 —

generally, to contribute as they can afford—to monument American valor and mark the hero remains of those who, almost unknown, in a hostile prison camp, ended their service to the cause in the grave?

Time has fortunately blunted the bitter feelings of hatred between the sections of the late civil war, a united country is enjoying prosperity, the people are happy, the soldiers of the Southern "battle cross" are now respected, certainly by those who crossed swords with them, and the government is anxious that the living comrades should properly mark the resting places of their dead Confederate associates and care for their graves and burial grounds!

Consequently, a donation is sought of the living to monument the dead; and, whomsoever desires should contribute according to the interest felt and substance possessed.

The undersigned contributes his services and bears the expense of travel, correspondence, etc., and guarantees that every cent subscribed to and received by him shall be expended toward the erection of the proposed monument and care of the said burial grounds. With that view he has made arrangements with "The Merchants Loan and Trust Company," one of the wealthiest banks of the city of Chicago, to receive and retain on deposit, bearing interest, to be computed and entered up monthly, all moneys that shall be subscribed for the above referred to purpose, and to pay out such funds, only, for work actually done, on proper checks drawn by the depositor when countersigned by the Chairman of the Auditing Committee having charge of the expenditures for the proposed monument. [See deposit contract below.]

It is estimated that a monument commensurate with the possibilities of collections made and to be obtained, and of such magnitude as will do credit to the cause, will cost, together with the expense of preparing the ground, etc., from twelve to fifteen thousand dollars, of which amount fifteen hundred dollars has already been collected and is held on deposit by the Treasurer of the Association [this money is the proceeds of a lecture by Gen. J. B. Gordon] and over two thousand dollars in addition, conditionally subscribed. It is therefore necessary to raise at least ten thousand dollars, and so soon as that shall be assured steps will be taken to have the monument made of durable granite, after an appropriate design, and erected in time for unveiling, during the period of the World's Columbian Exposition in 1893.

All donations should be accompanied with a roster of the donors, giving amounts subscribed by each opposite the proper name; and, all subscriptions (where it is possible), should be paid by check, draft or money order, made payable to the said "Merchants Loan and Trust Company," and be forwarded to the undersigned at Division Headquarters in the Exchange Building, Chicago, Ills.

Trusting that this appeal for co-operative aid will receive the support that its merits deserve, I have the honor to remain

Very truly and sincerely,   JNO. C. UNDERWOOD,
Major-General, Commanding.

P. S.—It is also proposed to raise funds by limited subscription, with which to care for the Confederate dead buried at other places within the territory comprising the Division District.

Approved:

JNO. B. GORDON, *General Commanding U. C. V.*

DEPOSIT CONTRACT.
THE MERCHANTS LOAN AND TRUST COMPANY.
INCORPORATED 1857.
CAPITAL AND SURPLUS $3,600,000.

J. W. DOANE, President.   ORSON SMITH, 2d V. Prest.
P. L. YOE, V. Prest.   F. C. OSBORN, Cashier.
                                           CHICAGO, Jan. 30, 1892.

To Whom This Shall Concern:

This is to certify, that Jno. C. Underwood, Major-General of the Division of the Northwest, U. C. V., has contracted to deposit in this bank all moneys that may be contributed for the purpose of caring for and ornamenting the burial grounds of Confederate soldiers who died in the prison camps Douglas, in Chicago, Ills ; Johnson's Island, near Sandusky, O.; Chase, at Columbus, O.; Morton, at Indianapolis, Ind., and those who died and lie buried near Cairo, Ills —upon the following terms and conditions, viz :

All such moneys are to be deposited to Jno. C. Underwood's credit as Major-General of the Division and will draw interest, which interest will be computed and entered up monthly, and such fund will be paid out only on his official check when countersigned by the Chairmen of the Auditing Committees of the Associations above named, authorized to supervise and sanction the expenditure of money for improving the said burial grounds, erecting appropriate monuments thereon, etc.   THE MERCHANTS LOAN AND TRUST COMPANY.

ATTEST :   [Signed]   J. W. DOANE, *President.*
.   [Signed]   F. C. OSBORN, *Cashier.*
[Stock quoted, " 272 bid."]

[The following is a classified transcript of discovered data, and errors, should there be any, are the fault of the Burial Registers and not of the compiler.]

STATISTICAL ROSTER.

SUMMARY OF THE KNOWN CONFEDERATE DEAD BURIED AT OAKWOODS CEMETERY.

From Alabama 485
" Arkansas 405
" Arizona 2
" Florida 24
" Georgia 322
" Kentucky 361
" Louisiana 78
" Missouri 26
" Mississippi 446
" North Carolina 397
" South Carolina 13
" Tennessee 747
" Texas 608
" Virginia 187

MISCELLANEOUS

From Forrest's Cavalry 10
" First Regiment, combined Tenn., Miss and Ala., 16
" Sundry Commands 190

Total 4,317

Compiled and classified individually, in companies and regiments, and by States, as follows:

ALABAMA.

Aggregate dead **485**, classified as follows:

INFANTRY.			
From	1st Regiment		100
"	2d	"	1
"	3d	"	17
"	4th	"	25
"	5th	"	7
"	6th	"	1
"	7th	"	11
"	8th	"	7
"	9th	"	2
"	11th	"	2
"	13th	"	1
"	14th	"	4
"	15th	"	1
"	16th	"	3
"	17th	"	32
"	18th	"	10
"	19th	"	7
"	20th	"	4
"	21st	"	6
"	22d	"	7
"	23d	"	5
"	24th	"	3
"	25th	"	2
"	26th	"	1
"	27th	"	40
"	28th	"	9
"	29th	"	24
"	30th	"	5
"	31st	"	3
"	32d	"	3
"	33d	"	11
"	34th	"	11
"	36th	"	6
"	37th	"	6
"	38th	"	2
"	39th	"	10
"	40th	"	2
"	41st	"	8

INFANTRY.			
From	42d Regiment		4
"	43d	"	2
"	44th	"	1
"	45th	"	7
"	46th	"	8
"	48th	"	1
"	49th	"	1
"	50th	"	2
"	51st	"	4
"	53d	"	1
"	54th	"	2
"	55th	"	3
"	56th	"	1
"	57th	"	13
"	58th	"	1
"	59th	"	1
"	63d	"	1
"	Unknown		5
"	Regulars		4

CAVALRY.

From	1st Regiment		5
"	3d	"	2
"	4th	"	2
"	8th	"	2
"	Coates'	"	2
"	Montgomery's Regiment		1

ARTILLERY.

From	1st Battery		1
"	3d	"	1
"	10th	"	1
"	Pickett's Battery		3
"	Sample's	"	1
"	Nelson's	"	3

DETAILS.

Name.	Co.	Reg't.	Name.	Co.	Reg't.
Adams, B.	F	18	Armstrong, Jas	F	1
Adams, J. H.	E	1	Adias, Thos. B.	B	37
Aubrey, Wm.	E	51	Armstrong, H. C.	C	17
Autery, Benj.	A	17	Akin, J. M.	C	39
Algood, J. W.	G	37	Akin, Silas M.	E	39
Addock, H.	D	29	Ainsworth, John	...	3 Cav.

Name.	Co.	Reg't.	Name.	Co.	Reg't.
Allen, Luther	K	29	Clarke, J	R	Pickett's Battery.
Adams, A. D	G	13			
Avery, Judson	...	Reg'r.	Crens, John S., or Crews	I	1
Braden, A. J	A	27	Chandler, Jesse	H	1 Cav.
Balcombe, Allen	C	27	Cotton, R	I	4 "
Borum, John S	D	27	Cockraft, Elick	G	15
Burke, Wm	D	27	Chadwick, John S	E	39
Beard, Jas. A	F	27	Chance, William A	A	33
Benton, Dan'l	F	21	Canterbury, O	B	20
Bigby, J. L	...	18	Clarke, F F	B	37
Brown, Isaiah	A	1 Bat'y.	Chambers, William F	C	7
Bunkley, L D	B	1	Creech, S. S	C	17
Byrne, Patrick	B	21	Cooper, William	E	34
Brown, W. N	G	18	Carson, John	D	39
Brook, J. W	K	27	Country, Salvador	...	30
Beasley, James	F	1	Castlebury, J. M	B	30
Bedingfield, James	I	27	Carpenter, John	B	30
Blue, A. D	G	1	Coker, Joseph	H	29
Brown, E F	K	1	Carr, J. E	A	57
Bardham, H	G	1	Champion, H	E	1
Blankenship, W. H	B	34	Calhoun, J. J	A	32
Baker, E	B	31	Cox, John B	H	29
Browning, S. W	F	8 Cav.	Clarke, Philip	C	40
Blackman, James H	H	1	Crump, Charles	...	... Bat'n.
Barnett, O A	H	4	Coyer, Joseph	D	4
Butler, T. R	B	33	Carroll, John	D	29
Brouthers, H. A	H	19	Cox, W. R	G	3
Butler, Benjamin	A	34	Courten, T. W		Samples' Bat.
Berry, William B	C	17	Cheatham, W. A	K	17
Brown, Anderson	G	57	Carmichael, C	H	16
Bocks, M. S	G	13	Cole, J. T	H	8
Brown, John	F	3	Cheek, Robert W	I	17
Brown, John	K	29	Chapman, George	D	22
Barnett, James	A	28	Collins, Robert	E	1
Ballenger, James	F	3	Crocker, D. W	H	1
Billingslee, A. A	I	46	Cousins, Frank	C	1
Barganier, W. J	K	17	Dunn, R. W	G	27
Brown, Nathaniel R	H	17	Dewberry, Jabez	A	27
Bigley, F. J	G	33	Davenport, J. W	E	1
Bracken, Robert	G	16	Dosier	...	...
Bragg, C. P	E	7	Davaughn, M	G	46
Bridges, A. G	D	28	Davis, S	H or K	25
Black, Robert M. or Robert L	D	33	Deas, J. B	B	51
			Durbin, H. S	D	29
Bonham, J. S	F	17	Dayton, J. C	E	45
Butler, Benjamin	A	3	Dean, Lewis	A	37
Burkett, William E	E	23	Dobson, Von G. B	B	22
Brooks, Joshua	...	19	Digger, James	G	57
Bowman, William J	A	8	Deans, W. H	B	17
Blackley, John	F	1	Duncan, J. B	I	... Inf'y.
Bowers, D	...	Reg'r	Derden, A. J	D	17
Blackburn, Benjamin	F	41	Dawdle, G A	K	56
Bradford, J. W	I	1	Dowday, A J	G	46
Braun, J. H	H	1	Davidson, David	F	45
Bloodworth, J	...	1	DePuyster, R.D. or R.F	G	1
Burke, W. R	...	1	Ennis, Eli	E	21
Beashey, James	F	1	Elkins, J. H	K	34
Carter, Wesley	C	3 Bat'n	Ellis, M. J	F	33
Christianson, Chas. J	C	21	Edwards, J. F	C	54
Cropp, W. D., or Croft	D	22	Echols, J	G	25
Cox, C. A or S. A	F	1	Edwards, William	D	6
Casey, G. B	D	17	Elliott, Alfred	B	17
Chaffin, J	B	27	Edins, J. S	H	18
Cheatham, G. W	C	1	Eaton, William	K	1
Cassen, J	I	39	Flint, J. C	C	27

Co.	Reg't.	Name	Co.	Reg't.
....	Coates' Cav'y.	Holdmen, C. W	K	17
.... F	1	Howell, E	G	41
.... E	7	Hallas, H	B	20
.... D	20	Hainsbay, John A	G	57
.... K	49	Henderson. J	H	29
.... G	55	Holland, D	K	17
.... B	36	Hitchcock, John	K	34
.... C	17	Hammond, T. B	H	...
.... F	4	Holden, James	F	37
.... H	1	Harris, William H	F	33
.... G	1	Hartford, William	A	1
.... K	27	Hagins, John	H	1
1.......... K	19	Hendricks, J. A	D	1
.... G	1	Isbral, E	E	29
.... E	1	Jones, C.	E	27
.... E	1	Jamerson, J. D	H	11
.... D	21	Jenkins, W. C	D	1 Cav.
.... G	41	Jones, William	F	11
.... H	19	Johnson, J. R	G	1
.... A	4	Johnson, A	E	58
.... K	53	Johnson, J. H	B	42
.... K	42	James, John	D	14
.... D	16	Johney, C. D, or Johnson	H	24
.... H	29	Johnson, S. D.	K	24
.... 1	17	Jacobs, A D.	G	43
.... B	17	Joyner, Willet N	H	4
.... C	1	Jones, F J	G	29
.... 1	26	Jones, Allen	B	18
.... C	36	Jones, C. F	D	8
.... C	28	Jones, W. H	B	37
.... K	27	Jones. John C	...	... Reg'r.
.... H	39	Jay, George	...	1
.... G	1	Jones, R. H	B	1
....	27	Koton, Archie	K	27
.... A	27	Kirkpatrick, J. A	C	1
.... K	17	Krena, Mitchell	B	1 Cav.
i.......... G	27	Keemoe, I	F	1
.... E	1	Kelly, John R	1	45
.... Nelson's Art.		Key, Dr	L	28
.... A	3	Kemp, S	F	4
·.......... C	1	Kenney, P	H	18
.... F	31	Kanada, J	K	1
.... G	28	Kinchen, A. J	G	1
.... A	31	Lawrence, Thomas or S. T	H	27
M. ..... F	4	Lee, Carter	1	1
mes E. D	4	Lyle, E. F	H	27
H........ F	33	Landley, C. L	1	18
M........ F	4	Lamb, W. W	H	34
r W. H. G	44	Long, Dick R	D	14
.... K	34	Linsey, J. M	D	48
.... G	41	Long, Thomas	B	39
as........ F	51	Lamb, William M	K	54
as........ K	42	Little, B H or B. F	H	20
B........ B	1	Lambert, W. H	C	4
o B...... D	33	Linsey, A. R	B	33
.... L	28	Leck, J. W	C	1
b........ I	45	Linsey, W. J	C	22
.... D	4	Lowery, James	D	1
mes...... C	55	McElroy, W. M	F	27
.... C	57	Morris, C. H	F	27
.... C	28	Mothershead, S. A	F	24
m F..... G	17	Miles, Frank	H	1
as H.... K	17	Moss, L. A	1	18
iam H.				
.... D	29			

Name.	Co.	Reg't.
Moore, L. D.	E	1
Mahoney, A. M.	D	27
Morgan, W. W.	A	27
Marshall, W. A.	A	3 Bat.
Morse, A. T.	Nelson's Art.	
Miller, W. R.	B	1
Morgan, J. B.	G	10 Bat'y.
Manu, John M.	A	4
Mason, J. W.	E or C	1
Morrow, J. W. or N. M.	D	5
Mun. Rollin N.	B	57
Matheney, J. F.	K	24
McDaniel, —.	H	39
McMin, John.	A	4
McHafey, William.	H	1
McCloud, William.	A	23
Mulberry, James.	B	45
McDaniel, J. C.	B	30
Moore, G. W.	C	46
Martin, William K.	G	5
McClelland, John.	D	29
Mason, John M.	H	17
Merrick, A. J.	G	16
Munson, J. L.	B	23
Morris, Jesse.	H	17
Mordwin, A.		38
Moran, C.	C	34
Morgan, James.	H	36
McIntrye, S. A.		38
Miller, John C.	D	29
McRae, John D.	1	29
McDonald, L. M.	E	51
Matthews, J.	A	14
Maize, William.		1 Cav.
McCloud, J. H.	D	57
Morris, N. C.	D	1
Middleton, J. B.	B	1
Morton, B.	G	1
Norris, C. H.	F	27
Nules, Thomas.	Nelson's Art.	
Newberry, W. T.	B	1
Neal, F. M.	A	19
Noblin, G. W.	G	33
Nothcutb, Elijah.	A	4
Nichols, Henry.	G	8
Nab or Nanabb, J. C.	H	22
Owen, Elijah.	K	19
Owen, J. R.	A	3
Okes, Charles W.	1	Montgomery's Bat.
Owen, S. A.	Pickett's Cav.	
O'Neil, C.	F	4
Pryor, D.	G	41
Prise, B.	E	1
Plennett, J.	G	9
Powell, Peter.	D	27
Patterson, E. S.	K	27
Philips, T. J.	A	3
Perry, F. A.	H	1
Pierce, G. W.	F	27
Peters, D. S.	F or E	1
Peek, H. C.	H	27
Perkins, G. W.	1	Morgan's Regular.
Prickett, J. W.	B	1

Name.	Co.	Reg't.
Pratt, James F.	H	50
Pratt, Jesse.	G	9
Philips, William B.	F	23
Parks, M. G.	A	57
Prewett, F. M.	G	17
Parker, John.	A	28
Parker, G. G.	G	17
Perkins, H. O.	H	8
Patrick, William.	G	57
Pedigo, J. W.	1	29
Paine, William.	K	17
Pride, R. J.	E	5
Poe, Payton.	B	5
Prickett, Thomas.	K	36
Prosser, Isaiah.	H	5
Perry, George W.	A	39
Price, W. H.	C	63
Pless, James.	G	34
Quillebaum, Wilkes.	A	57
Quinn, M.	B	1
Ryan, Isaac.	H	27
Rutlege, R. F.	H	27
Read, J. D.	C	3
Rhodes, R.	H	33
Russell, James.	B or D	14
Roper, Harrison.	1	4
Roberts, F. C. or T. C.	E	7
Rogers, H. R.	C	46
Rizar, L.	C	46
Reynolds, G. W.	G	8
Rhea, Richard.		
Reeves, C. J.	H	7
Robertson, W. G.	1	18
Rhodes, J. C.	D	57
Rent, William.	Pickett's Ba	
Richardson, H. W.	G	1
Read, W.	K	1
Ragan, J. B.	H	1
Rannall, J.	H	1
Rainwater, P.	D	1
Raudell, F.	H	1
Register, William.	D	1
Roten, Archie.	K	27
Rigby, J. L.		18
Story, James.	C	3
Stratton. H.	C	3
Sherrin, Anthony.	K	1
Sanders, Wiley.	A	1
Smith, W. B.	A	17
Stinson, A. J.	E	1
Strickland, W. J. or W. T.	A	3
Smoot, A. A.	G	1
Strickland, M. A.	F	1
Senn, (S.) N.	E	1
Slaughter, R.	1	41
Spiney, E.	G	1
Stokes, W. W. or W. H.	1	1
Standland, T. M.	E	1
Scott, Thomas.	B	1
Saunders, D.	E	17
St. John, W. W.	C	41
Smith, A. F.	D	4
Sparks, E. P.	D	4
Swords, Shilton.	1	4

Name.	Co.	Reg't.
Sublett, George	G	4
Smith, Solomon B.	B	7
Strothar, W. D.	A	39
Steyall, Reuben	F	17
Smith, M.	E	29
Smyley, William	H	36
Snyder, Solomon.	C	46
Seebs, A. J.	F	27
Shaw, Robert H.	G	55 Cav.
Strickland, S. J.	A	29
Surratt, Jacob	G	1
Stewart, C. W.	E	1
Saunders, William		1
Suggerough, J.	C	1
Stewart, W. C. or W. G.	D	3
Senn, L.	F	1
Smith, A.	C	1
Spears, H. W.	B	1
Tansry, J. R.		3
Talbott, M. H.	A	1
Thomas, George	G	19
Tomlinson, William	E	1
Tamplin, J. H.	H	1
Thomas, G. W.	I	1 Cav.
Tlonee, E.	G	41
Tate, Samuel	D	4
Thompson, T. J.	B	8 Cav.
Toney, John	F	4
Thenemore, T.	D	5
Tatterson, James S. E.	D	3
Taylor, Richard	G	27
Thomas, D.	B	7
Taylor, John	A	17
Trumbull, G. W.	H	7
Tripp, J. C.	I	5
Trice, A.	C	45
Thornton, R. D.	H	59
Tollis, John	B	39
Thompson, P. H.	K	1
Taylor, Milton	D	1
Unknown	F	4
Vaun, James	I	1
Vernon, Obadiah	K	17
Vaughn, J. W.	B	17
Vaughn, J. C.	K	7
Williams, S. A.	I	27
Wesson, William	C	27

Name.	Co.	Reg't.
Winsted, S.	A	3
Watkins, Julius	H	1
Watson, S. F.	C	3 Bat'n.
Wood, A. M.	D	27
Wilson, P. H.	K	27
Williams, G. R.	F	1
Wilson, William	G	27
Wall, S. J.	F	1
Walthal, E. P.	B or E	1
Wells, William	I	29
Watkins, R. H.	B	3 Cav.
Wallace, S.	F	34
Wiggins, J. A.	H	32
Walker, R. M.	F	4
White, B. F.	B	4 Cav
Ward, J. W.	B	1 Cav.
Williams, W. C.	C	1
Williams, H. J.	B	2 Bat'n 1st Legion
Woosley, John	C	50
Wiggins, J. H.	B	32
Watkins, Calvin	K	36
Wright, Levi	F	57
Wittow, H. C.	H	29
Whitney, S.	F	42
Whatley, Willie	B	23
Wall, S. W.	G	29
Williams, B. F.	I	45
Williams, James O.	F	28
Wilkins, O. T.		Coates' State Guards.
Woodew, John	B	22
White, Andrew	F	57
Whatley, A. J.	K	22
Williams, R.	I	29
Wood, W. E.	B	7
Wright, W. J.	G	7
Wildes, William	I	29
Whittle, H. H.	B	1
Woodward, A. H.	K	1
Walker, J.	H	30
Watson, A. R.	I	1
Yarborough, G. W. or S. W.	F	27
Young, W. E.	A	34
Yates, Peter	A	40

ARKANSAS

Aggregate dead **405**, classified as follows:

INFANTRY.

From 1st Regiment			9
" 2d	"		10
" 3d	"		4
" 4th	"		3
" 5th	"		2
" 6th	"		6
" 7th	"		1
" 8th	"		12
" 9th	"		1
" 11th	"		92
" 12th	"		20
" 13th	"		4
" 14th	"		2
" 15th	"		7
" 16th	"		1
" 17th	"		3
" 18th	"		1
" 19th	"		145
" 23d	"		1
" 24th	"		26
" 33d	"		1
" 39th	"		1

INFANTRY.

From 42d Regiment			
" 45th	"		
" 62d	"		
Unknown			
Conscript			
Citizen			
Indian Chief			

CAVALRY.

From Branenburg Cavalry

ARTILLERY.

From Crawford's Battery	
" Dunnington's Naval Battery	
" Hadley's Battery	
" Cox's Battery	
" Howard's 3d Battery	
" 2d Battery	
Unknown	

ENGINEERS.

From Sappers and Miners

DETAILS.

Name.	Co.	Reg't.	Name.	Co.	Reg't.
Atkinson, Thomas L...	G	8	Brabbin, G. W.	C	4
Alaway, W. W.	B	11	Brook, B. L.	A	Crawford Battery.
Alton, E.	E	11			
Answorth, R. F.	E	4	Box, James		Detached Naval Bat.
Answorth, A. G.	C	24			
Anderson, Jno. or Ph.	I	19	Barker, P. or A. P.	E	19
Anderson, Jackson	E	19	Brown, T.	H	19
Almond, Daniel	D		Barber, Noah W.	E	24
Anderson, R A	...	2 Batt'y.	Benton, W. J	E	24
Burnett, J. E.	H	11	Burnet, R. H.	F	19
Burgess, W. M.	I	11	Bell, J.	C	19
Brown, W. J.	H	11	Brown, Benjamin	F	19
Barnes, J.	E	11	Bibb, Allen	F	19
Bevers, John	A	15	Batchelor, R.	I	19
Beesley, T. W.	E	11	Branch, Needham	I	19
Baety, A.	I	12	Burke, J. R.	B	Crawford Battery.
Beaty, R. T.	H	11			
Bussell, J. N.	G	11	Banks, James	B	24
Bleasol, C. H.	F	12	Brazier, James	C	19
Barrett, C. F.	F	12	Ballard, W.		Dunnington Naval Batt'y
Brewer, Joseph	B	11			

Name.	Co.	Reg't.
Baker, James	H	8
Byles, M. J	I	2
Bone, A. M	I	8
Bradford, David	D	39
Bailey, T	E	6
Burke, J. R	B	Crawford's Battery.
Bailey, R. T	H	11
Baker, John	C	8
Bledson, C. H	F	12
Brockett, E. M	E	11
Burke, T	F	19
Cox, S H	E	11
Carson, J. S	E	11
Copeland. A J	D	2
Chandler, J. R	I	19
Creed, William N	B	Crawford's Battery.
Clement, William	A	14
Craig, John O. or J. E.	I	19
Cook, J. M	A	21
Cooper, W. H	D	19
Cary, Thomas	C	19
Chassier, Z	C	19
Chandler, J. E	E	19
Campbell, A	C	19
Cheany, H. W	A	24
Conley, James	B	19
Campbell, A. J	H	19
Clarke, Joseph	H or F	19
Cockman, B. or D	B	11
Cooper, J. F	G	2
Conner, G. W	D	8
Craig, John	I	8
Coleman, T. C	C	5
Conrad, John M	B	2
Conger, John	B	6
Copeland, H. D	D	2
Cox, T. C		Crawford's Battery.
Cannon, G. W	D	8
Charley, "servant"		Dunnington's Battery.
Caster, John		Sappers and Miners.
Dempsey, J	H	11
Davis, B. F	K	12
Davenport, H. J	F	19
Dowell, John	A	Cox's Batt'y
Draper, Milton M	1	19
Dobbs, S. J	I	19
Daniels, Silas	E	16
Dougherty, John	K	24
Doland, James	F	19
Dorvell, J		Sappers and Miners.
Dorson, H	G	12
Davenport, A. W	E	11
Dasison, U. M	G	12
Elliot, G. W	G	11
Etheridge, B. J	D	11
Elliot, G. B	E	12
Eddy, James	C	19
Edings, Isaac	A	19
Elliot, Andrew	B	1
Egner, E	I	8
Evans, F. V		Naval Batt'y.
Evans, T. N		" "
Fuller, James		15
Fulighain, Josiah	B	11
Forsyth, H. L	B	11
Flindale, J. W	B	19
Fuckner, R	D	17
Faye, L. K	I	24
Fox, T C	B	Crawford's Battery.
Furgerson, B	B	21
Fisher, A	A	19
Fuller, J	F	19
French, G. W	F	19
Farron, Elias M	I	19
Flanigan, Andrew F.	F	19
Fitch, William	B	6
Frey, I. L	I	24
Gray, A. H	H	11
Gregg, John E		Crawford's Battery.
Goodson, S. T	B	19
Gorgan, C	I	13
Goodwin, W. D	F	19
Glass, H	H	19
Garman, P. J	A	19
Gibess, William A	F	24
Gillespie, W. C	A	2
Giles, William A	F	21
Gibbon, J. B	A	11
Gill, W. O		Crawford's Battery.
Greggory, J. P	E	19
Hamilton, J. C	A	12
Homan, John	B	11
Hindman, F. M	H	11
Haddon, E. C	G	11
Horton, A	A	11
Harris, E. C	A	12
Humphrey, W. W	D	12
Herron, N	I	11
Harville, J. J	B	11
Hall, J. B	B	11
Herron, G. M. or J. M.	G	7
Hutchinson, T. J	B	11
Hardy, J. F	H	11
Huddon, William M		Sappers.
Hall, William	I	19
Hargrass, William	F	19
Hansley, Josiah	F	19
Hill, M. J	C	19
Hiburn, J. M	E	1
Harnett, John D	A	19
Holt, Jesse	I	19
Highfield, Smith	H	19
Hendricks, R	H	19
Halley, R. H	H	19
Huffman, A. A. or A. J.	A	19
Herring, C. M	D	4
Harper, J. S	I	3
Holloway, W. H	A	4
Hedge, A	D	23
Henial, Robert	F	19
Jackson, R. J	I	11

Name.	Co.	Reg't.
Jameson, William	H	11
Jackson, J. W	E	11
Jones, J. N	I	8
Jackson, J. W	B	13
Johnson, Henry	F	2
Joiner, W. L	B	8
Johnson, Wm. H	Sappers and Miners.	
Jones, William	F	11
Jameson, John	H	11
Kaighton, S. G	C	11
Kinsey, Peter	I	11
Kiskers, J. M	I	11
Kates, Benjamin F	A	12
King, A	B	11
Keller, William	B	19
King, John	A	Crawford's Battery.
Kunzee, A W., "Indian Chief"		
Keith, Robert		Art'y.
Kenway, J. A. F		19
Kizzier, T. J	A	19
Kelow, Thomas W	K	1
Lancier, P	H	11
Lewis, H W. or W. H.	E	11
Lucas, Thomas	A	11
Lawrence, Benton or Newton	B	11
Love, W. B	A	12
Lewis, George R	E	11
Lewis, E. T	E	11
Lyons, J	I	13
Lord, Robert P	E	19
Lunn, H. J	D	19
Lemons, A	I	24
Letting, Charles	Dunnington's Naval Batt'y.	
Langford, John	2 Batt'y.	
Lowe, W. B	A	12
Murdock, C. P	Crawford's Battery.	
McAltie, Thomas B	G	19
McGill, James S	E	11
Moton, T. C	D	19
Mowers, Thomas H	Crawford's Artillery.	
Merritt, J G	B	1
Markland, Nimrod	2	
Morris, Thomas H	A	Crawford's Artillery.
Milligan, J. R	B	11
Merrit, M. L	E	11
Magill, James E	I	11
Mason, J. W. or J. M	K	12
(Mc A. J.) McDonald, A. J	B	11
Miller, J. R	A	11
McMahan, J. A	K	12
McKinney, James A	F	11
Morton, E. C	B	11
Meader, J. W	E	11
McCarty, William	I	12
Massey, John M	E	11
Massey, L. P	E	11

Name.	Co.	Reg't.
Moreland, H	A	2
McKown, Jasper (colored)	I	19
Measles, D. C	E	24
Mayton, Nathan	H	19
Mayber, Henry	I	19
McClure, A. W	C	19
Malone, J. M	I	19
Mitchell, R. H	E	24
McAltie, George B	E	19
Mealbreth, John	H	19
Morgan, A. S	E	19
Meatle, Thomas	G	19
May, John N	E	19
Meater, William C	E	19
McDonald, O	I	24
Mayber, R. S	G	19
Moore, Joseph E	H	19
Magby, Charles	C	19
Millau, D. M, or McMillan	E	19
Murren, J. C	E	21
McDowell, Robert	F	19
Murroon, J. A	C	19
Marberry, Peter	C	19
McFarland, J. F	B	19
Mosely, B. G	F	24
Mosely, W. A	F	24
Megrough, J. C	A	19
Merrill, Benjamin S	I	19
Mitchell, William C	F	14
Mason, W. L	E	17
McDonald, Robert	F	19
Moore, J. H	H	19
Mow, Benjamin	F	19
McAltie, W. H	E	19
Marshall, W. A		Bat'n
Marres, J	F	3
Nichols, J. H	A	11
Newkirk, W. R	F	11
Newman, John	B	15
Nelson, James	F	19
Newton, T. C	D	19
Night, J	A	24
Nelson, William	B	19
Nelson, David	I	19
Nash, G. J	Crawford's Battery.	
ONeil, E. W	E	19
Ober, Sylvestus	A	Cox's Bat.
Owens, R	F	19
Owens, G. W	A or B	1
Oxford, T. J	F	19
O'Richey, —		19
Permine, B. F	I	11
Perrins, E	G	11
Perator, L. E	C	15
Phillips, William	I	11
Pitts, John	F	11
Page, James	F	11
Paster, F. D	C	19
Perkins, J	F	19
Payne, John R	F	19
Patton, David	C	19
Perrion, W. H	G	45

Name.	Co.	Reg't.
Pitman, B.	I	24
Peppersmall, J W.	F	19
Polk, James C.	A	24
Purchett, J. N.	F	19
Philips, T. V.	I	19
Parker, Ransom.	F	19
Pritchard, John.	G	19
Parker, William M.	I	24
Poole, Richard P.		Reg'r.
Pann, B.	Norman Co.	
Philipps, J. V.	I	19
Phess, A.		
Porter, F. D.	C	19
Paton, James.	C	19
Rose, Pinckney R.	A	15
Rufter, G. W.	I	11
Raswell, R.	D	11
Rowan, William.	B	11
Reynolds, W. K. P.	E	11
Rucker, S. M.	F	12
Reynolds, B. E.	A	11
Rockett, E. M.	E	11
Rogers, W. F.	F	11
Rains, R.	K or D	3
Russell, John.	I	19
Robinson, James.	K	19
Robinson, John S.	K	19
Renberry, James F.	F	19
Rhodes, T. F. or L. F.	B	19
Rose, Elbert J., or Roe.	B	19
Rivers, A. J.	B	19
Robinson, W. M.	C	19
Rhodes, L. L.	B	19
Raines, Samuel.	D Shafer's.	
Ramsey, William.	A	11
Russell, J. M.	G	11
Rutley, W. A., or Rutlege.	B Crawford's Artillery.	
Raing, John.	Crawford's Battery.	
Spear, James.	I	11
Strange, G. J.	H	11
String, G. W.	F	11
Scofield, John.	F	11
Snodgrass, W. P.	B	11
Shepard, William S.	A	11
Sloan, James.	C	11
Speers, Julius.	C	11
Sanford, T. J.	A	15
Smith, W. V. or M. V.	G	2
Shaw, Thomas.	Conscript.	
Sides, C. W.	B	19
Steward, John A.	A Crawford's Battery.	
Sandback, William.	A J. Branenburg Cav.	
Stanley, James.	B	19
Shepard, Labum.	3 Bat. Howard Legion.	
Stewart, John C.	I	19
Southward, R.	Sappers and Miners.	
Stewart, William.	D	42
Sewell, John W.	A	24

Name.	Co.	Reg't.
Stout, A. J. or A. T.	H	19
Stuart, John.	H	19
Sanders, William.	G	19
Skinner, Jesse.	F	19
Starr, John.	H	19
Strandle, S. Y.	B	19
Sanders, Matthew.	E	5
Saunders, H. C.	D	62
Snowdy, G. R.	B	19
Shuttlewort, J. C.	I	6
South, James.	F	33
Seitz, Davidson.	K	3
Simmons, A. F.	L	1
Saunders, William.	G	17
Sill, William O.	B Crawford's Battery.	
Smith, Joseph.	Crawford's Battery.	
Thomas, Samuel.	H	11
Turrentine, D. A.	G	12
Tite, W.	B	6
Turquett, J. M.	B	19
Treadwell, D. C.	B Crawford's Battery.	
Tucker, W. H.	H	19
Thornton, R. T.	B	19
Thompson, J. M.	H	19
Turentine, A.	B	19
Trotter, T. C.	F	19
Turner, J.	G	21
Townsend, J. A.	D	19
Tabor, G. W.	F	19
Tidnier, James F.	B	19
Tyre, Robert.	E	19
Taylor, C. M.	F	19
Taylor, John.	I	8
Trevatoe, L. E.	C	15
Todd, T. J.	G	11
Taber, George W.	F	18
Trolind, J. H. or Trolinder.	K	11
Upton, Peter.	D	1
Vaughn, E. W.	H	11
Waters, F. M.	A	11
Waters, J. W.	H	11
Williamson, W. M.	B	11
Welsh, George.	Hadley's Bat.	
Watson, J. W.	A	11
Watkins, William A.	E	11
Whisenhunt, William.	G	12
Webb, Norman.	B	11
Walker, W. H.	D	8
Whittender, W. H.	E	19
Woodruff, M.M.or N.M.	Detached Naval Battery.	
Williams, S. L. or L. S.	E	19
Wilson, C.	E	19
Wallace, John.	E	19
Williams, Rollin or Rowlin.	F	19
Weaver, James K.	F	19
White, Benjamin.	F	19
Watson, D. M.	C	19
Walker, Brown.	A Crawford's Battery.	

Name.	Co.	Reg't.	Name.	Co.	Reg't.
Wyatt, M. D.	A	Confederate Bat'y	Ward, M.	F	9
Whitehead. S. W.	E	24	Young, W. J.	G	13
Wilson, James	B	19	Young, James H.	E	19
Willard, Herman	H	19	Yondale, James	H	19
Willis, F H	K	1	Yandall, John	H	19
Williams, B. F.	B	1	Yandem, W. W.	H	19

GEORGIA.

Aggregate dead **322**, classified as follows:

INFANTRY.				INFANTRY.		
From 1st Regiment		24		From 53d Regiment		1
" 2d	"	8		" 54th	"	3
" 3d	"	2		" 55th	"	98
" 4th	"	6		" 56th	"	4
" 5th	"	5		" 57th	"	3
" 6th	"	7		" 62d	"	3
" 8th	"	6		" 63d	"	11
" 9th	"	2		" 64th	"	2
" 15th	"	1		" 65th	"	11
" 16th	"	11		" 66th	"	5
" 22d	"	1		" Cox's Legion		2
" 23d	"	1		" State Guards		1
" 25th	"	3		" R. R. Guards		1
" 27th	"	2		" Reserves		2
" 29th	"	7		Unknown		1
" 30th	"	10		Citizen		1
" 32d	"	1				
" 33d	"	2		**CAVALRY.**		
" 34th	"	4		From 1st Regiment		3
" 35th	"	4		" 3d	"	1
" 36th	"	3		" 4th	"	1
" 37th	"	12		" 5th	"	2
" 39th	"	5		" 6th	"	1
" 40th	"	4				
" 41st	"	2		**ARTILLERY.**		
" 42d	"	7		From 1st Battery		2
" 43d	"	5		" 8th "		1
" 44th	"	2		" 10th "		1
" 45th	"	1		" Burns' Battery		2
" 46th	"	3		" Crofts' "		1
" 47th	"	3		Unknown		1
" 52d	"	3				

DETAILS.

Name.	Co.	Reg't.		Name.	Co.	Reg't.
Argo, John	K	55		Brooks, John B	...	...
Ashburn, William	C	6		Bell, H. W	11	8
Adams, F. M	G	55		Bishop, Ephraim	E	2
Acock, H. I.	A	8		Barrenton, Silas	H	55
Brown, W. L.	B	55		Briggs, Henry	I	1
Burd, William	I	55		Bell, E. M	G	55
Brooks, B. F.	E	55		Burnes, John	G	1
Boyle, J. B	D	55		Blalock, W. B.	B	8
Blanks, S. S.	I	30		Brown, T. F.	D	63
Brown, David	D	55		Bates, Wilson	E	55
Backus, William	F	55		Blake, William.	C	62
Brown, R. C.	K	35		Blitch, J T	I	54
Bell, William H	D	2		Boozill, H	C	65

Name.	Co.	Reg't.
Brantley, N. G.	G	4
Brown, Benjamin	B	1
Brown, Daniel	B	55
Brand, John	I	16
Bell, John J.	H	55
Curley, N. M.	I	65
Cram, C. M.	H	4
Cannon, Peter	Citizen.	
Clouts, J. M.	C	1 Legion
Casson, Eli	E	25
Culbreth, J. E.	A	55
Crowroft, C. C.	B	55
Colclough, J. T.	D	55
Cross, A. J.	C	55
Cook, James A.	D	55
Crane, Charles N.	H	4
Chaflin, C. L.	B	37
Chandler, Daniel W.	G	42
Calahan, J. H.	B	55
Cook, C. C.	E	36
Clarke, C. A.	I	43
Chasten, C. B.	C	42
Carroll, James E.	F	4
Calvines, W. B.	B	2
Carroll, J. D.	D	55
Cueter, William	I	27
Carter, William C.	C	43
Conan, E.	E	25
Carson, John	D	56
Cockraft, Charles	B	55
Casey, R. R.	G	3
Dodger, W. J.	Burns' Batt'y.	
Davis, A. L.	K	55
Durden, J. E.	A	55
Derrick, Charles	A	1 Cav.
Davis, E.	F	34
Davis, J. A.	D	55
Dunton, D. N.	B	36
Daniels, G. W.	H	1
Dunaway, F. C.	H	37
Dodd, William	G	55
Davis, W. W.	I	16
Duncan, C. B.	B	37.
Dail, Patrick	G	55
Eardley, A. G.	C	30
Elmore, John	C	1 Cav.
Ellison, T. D.	A	1
Elson, John	E	29
Eldridge, William	B	55
Faubrough, J. S.	A	9
Fain, J. A. L.	K	2 Cav.
Feen, F. W.	C	16
Farmer, F. F.	B	30
Flannigan, Elijah	D	16
Foshee, John W.	F	22
Famlin, F. M.	A	1
Foster, E. H.	A	1
Ford, J.	G	40
Freeman, John T.	I	55
Grice, James	A	55
Gamer, J.	D	1 Batt'y.
Green, Oliver	D	35
Gillard, M.	G	29
Garner, W. W. W.	I	55
Goswell, Thomas T.	D	43

Name.	Co.	Reg't.
Gain, Moses	C	41
Grow, Nathaniel H.	A	43
Griffin, A. F.	D	63
Gandy, James Y.	B	56
Gordan, C. B.	E	46
Griffin, W. H.	H	1 Batt'y.
Georges, J. J.	A	8
Green, G. G.	E	8
Goldow, John F.	B	55
Garren, John	D	1
Galaway, William J.	A	55
Gray, F. M.	K	37
Hawkes, John	K	39
Hampton, C.	H	55
Honecutt, M. R.	I	55
Head, C.	E	65
Haynes, J. B.	D or H	30
Henry, J. T.	B	35
Herring, A. O.	G	55
Hodges, James	D	55
Hall, C. A.	G or C	55
Hooper, W.	G	65
Horton, Thomas R.	K	15
Heufner, Richard	G	41
Hicks, James P.	A	64
Horthom, William	E	55
Hardy, S. H.	I	66
Harris, Edwin	H	55
Hurley, Henry W.	I	2
Hopper, John A.	K	37
Hine, William H. or William A.	E	30
Horton, John	I	46
Hunt, W. H.	G or D	37
Hearwell, James H.	D or G	16
Hyde, Henry	I	37
Herviant, S. J.	F	63
Herry, J.	H	57
Hart, Joseph D.	C	45
Honegh, M. R.	I	55
Hall, James B.	A	44
Henry, John B.	B	55
Jones, A. S.	I	32
Jenkins, John.	K	55
Jackson, N. A.	K	55
Johson, N. A.	K	55
Johnston, E.	B	55
Jackson, R.	H	55
Joyce, William	H	55
Jenks, C. S.	K	1
Jenkins, C. S.	K	1
Johnson, Benjamin	H	55
Johnson, A. J.	H	65
Jackson, John E.	E	6 Cav.
Johnson, C.	I	5
Johnson, Joseph J.	K	1 Res.
Jordan, E. R.	B	55
Johnson, L.	I	4 Cav.
Johnson, John A.	B	3
Knight, Calvin	B	16
Kimball, Thomas	H	6
King, Adam B.	A	9
Kutter, William	I	27
Kerscher, W. H.	C	36

Name.	Co.	Reg't.
Kennedy, J. B.	K	33
Kennedy, Lewis	K	33
Kilby, H. N.	A	1 Leg'n.
Lamberts, J.	Crofts' Batt'y.	
Lenther, J W	D	55
Lawrence, James	E	37
Lewis, J. O.	D	6
Lynn, J. E	A	6
Lamb, Uriah	A	42
Lowery, J. P.	C	6
Logan, J. M.	G	57
Lovell, J. W	G	55
Langdon, John H.	E	52
Luther, J M	D	55
McCarty, J.	Burns' Batt'y.	
Murphy, P.	F	37
Mays, William	1	55
McCarthy, B.	A	47
Moore, J. J	E	55
Moss, James P	D	55
Manning, A.	A	55
Moore, J. W.	1	55
McEduff, W.	1	55
Millirons, W. W.	11	35
Marshall, W. M	G	55
Martin, J. F.	D	55
Murray, S. G.	B	29
Mercer, Austin	...	1
McCorelkle, John	11	37
McLain, William G.	E	1
Mute, William	C	63
Mays, R. M.	F	55
Murray, R. L.	K	63
Mayton, John L	A	4
Manning, M	C	39
Montgomery, J.	D	52
Mins, John G.	G	37
McIntosh, A. W.	F	62
Murray, James	A	40
Moody, John B.	D	5 Cav.
Maxwell, F.	II	16 Bat.
McDonald, G. M.	B	29
McDaniel, C.	...	16 Bat.
Mack, John P.	B	63
Murt, J. L.	C	5
Massey, William B.	A	30
McDowell, John.	D	37
Maxwell, Thomas	B	1
Martin, R. C.	C	66
McCarty, Newton	1	65
Marshall A.	H	54
Morrison, T.	C	55
Mashmurn, John	C	55
Munhar, P.	N	1
Moon, W.	1	55
Note, W.	C	63
Nesmith, A.	K	47
Nichols, William	G	55
Nix, J C.	1	55
Newton, Thomas J	F	55
Page, J. M.	D	1
Philips, E.	C	55
Pieree, J. A.	A	55
Perry, James M	1	55
Pearce, Andrew	F	55

Name.	Co.	Reg't.
Peacock, H. G.	G	55
Perry, W. A.	I	55
Perry, G. L.	C	63
Page, J. L.	D	3 Cav.
Polland, W. P.	1	2
Pearse, L. M.	H	1
Parker, James	D	2
Porter, J. G.	A	52
Parks, William	E	16
Pate, H. M. R	E	66
Peterson, Nathan	H	55
Parsons, William	G	41
Philips, R.	C	5
Quick, W.	H	55
Quick, George	A	5 [G'ds.
Roberts, E. B.	E	1 State
Roberts, N.	R. R. Guards.	
Rhodes, J	B	65
Rigby, William	E	29
Roberts, J. L.	F	55
Robins, James	E	25
Ruderford, James L.	C	30
Randolph, Thomas	11	16
Robinson, A. D.	D	55
Rapp, Francis	F	30
Roberts, J. B	F	40
Roberts, William E.	G	23
Riskett, William	B	1
Rogers, E.	H	41
Sewell, M	B	1 Cav.
Smith, J. B.	I	55
Smith, Burrell	E	39
Sharper, W. W.	Cox's Leg'n.	
Simmons, R. S.	Cox's Leg'n.	
Smeat, G. W.	1	55
Smith, S. N.	D	47
Short, F. M.	C	55
Sovell, J. W.	G	55
Smith, Caleb.	G	55
Spears, D.	C	29
Smith, James	II	1
Stephens, J. M.	E	30
Suggs, W. A	C	1
Stone, S. J.	C	64
Singleton, John.	A	42
Segars, F. J	D	16
Saconi, D.	I	1
Spence, James	I	62
Swearing, John W.	E	55
Scale, B. C.	I	54
Simmons, H. B.	F	43
Stone, Philip.	F	63
Suggs, John.	A	34
Spark, Leonard	E	66
Shephard, J. J.	D	42
Sullivan, E. or M.	E	65
Strainge, F. or T.	D	34
Shepard, William M.	...	42
Silas, ——	C	55
Stone, A. O.	I	55
Spunrite, J. F.	H	39
Selt, J. A	B	55
Sweet, G. W.	1	55
Scroggins, Richard	G	29
Taunton, T. J.	E	57

Name.	Co.	Reg't.	Name.	Co.	Reg't.
Thrash, J. T.	K	55	Winney, K	K	63
Timmersman, ——	K	55	Walker, J. William	F	55
Turney, James	C	46	Washburn, John	E	55
Thrasher, Albert	C	66	Wings, W. B.	D	55
Tumben, F. C.	D	1	Woutham, Thomas J.	D	65
Tennon, David	F	5	Wright, James W.	D	8
Toups, Henry	G	30	Wood, G.	A	39
Thompson, P. R.	A	55	Whaley, J. D.	F	2
Teeters, J. M.	B	1 Bat.	Wolton, J. W.		56
Turner, E. J.	E	42	Williams, G. W.	B	63
Truncum, J. A.		55	Wadkins, W.	C	55
Vaught, G.	E	4	Wilkinson, J. J.	F	34
Vaughn, J. S.	H	6	Waldham, E. R.	I	5 Cav.
Vincent, Daniel	D	56	Woodward, S. J.		10 Batt'y.
VanDrelt, N.	H	6	White, William W.	B. Reserves.	
Wells, John	E	55	Williams, William	H	55
Weight, J. W.	D	8 Batt'y.	Youngblood, W. J.		... Batt'y.
Worthum, S.	D	65	Yackerman, E.	C	65
Whaler, J.	F	55	Zimmerman, John	K	55

KENTUCKY.

Aggregate dead **361**, classified as follows:

INFANTRY.		CAVALRY	
From 1st Regiment	5	From 1st Regiment	1
" 2d "	41	" 2d "	20
" 3d "	22	" 3d "	12
" 4th "	7	" 4th "	1
" 5th "	18	" 5th "	12
" 6th "	24	" 6th "	18
" 7th "	18	" 7th "	21
" 8th "	15	" 8th "	25
" 10th "	49	" 10th "	18
" 11th "	1	" 14th "	4
" 12th "	1	" 17th "	1
" 13th "	1	" Falkner's Regiment	1
" 14th "	12	" Clark's "	1
" 17th "	1	Unknown	1
" 18th "	1		
" Ward's "	1	ARTILLERY.	
" Brewer's Company	1	From Byrne's Battery	4
Unknown	2	" Hanley's "	1

DETAILS.

Name.	Co.	Reg't.	Name.	Co.	Reg't.
Armstrong, John	A	2	Blackstone, J. T.	A	10
Atwood, R. L.	A	2	Bryan, E. T.	A	8
Averitt, E. B.	G	10	Bell, N. A.	H	7
Austin, A. J.	C	10	Byasso, E.	A	2
Alvery, W. P.	F	10 Cav.	Berry, J. H.	G	8 Cav.
Allen, John	D	7	Brandon, M. F.	E	5 "
Anderson, H. K.	B	7 Cav.	Barnett, Ambros.	G	2 "
Adams, George	G	3	Bowers, Daniel		Falkner's Cavalry.
Allen, J. W.	K	10			
Anderson, G. W.	G	10	Bird, Thomas N.	C	8 Cav.
Amstead, Joseph	C	8	Butler, J. W.	B	5 "
Ashbell, John	B	2	Beard, J. R.	A	14
Athison, J	B	4	Brock, . M.	G	2
Barnett, Joshua	H	4	Braskers, John	H	10
Baldwin, D. M.	H	3	Bradley, J. A.	F	4
Berby, A. W.	H	8	Barren. ——	B	2
Bruce, E.	I	6 Cav.	Bowen, W. H.	H	5
Bogle, R G	H	6 "	Barton, W. R.	H	7
Berry, S. W.	B	7 "	Beauchamp, Samuel	E	6 Cav.
Brown, L. R.	B	6 "	Birchfield, N. G.	C	10
Besbell, J. A.	B	2 "	Bennett, James H.	...	5
Borser, W. R.	H	5 "	Beale, A. L.	G	8
Blackwell, H., shot in prison		Ward's Reg.	Boyle, W. H.	H	10
			Brusley, James	G	10
Barnes, William	B	10 Cav.	Barrett, B.	B	6

Name.	Co.	Reg't.
Bennett, W. H.	B	10
Bailey, John	B	6
Burnett, J.	H	4
Cole, J. B.	C	2
Coppace, W.	B	5 Cav.
Camper, A.	I	6
Copeland, J.	G	2 Cav.
Combs, I.	G	...
Cooke, J. J.	C	10 Cav.
Cook, James G.	H	6 "
Climers, James	D	7 "
Cullens, Marshall	F	10
Colliers, J. C.	A	10
Crump, C.		Byrne's Batt'y.
Croweklin, J. M.	G	8 Cav.
Connoy, John	G	8
Coal, William C.	C	10
Comfort, G. H.	L	2 Cav.
Clarke, James L.	D	8 "
Cammon, W. A.	D	10 "
Creswell, L. D.	D	14 "
Catlett, James H.	H	5
Ceil, J. H.	K	18
Coons, David E.	A	8 Cav.
Chambers, M. C.	G	2
Crumbrough, C.	F	5 Cav.
Cromwell, N. M.	F	10
Cooper, J. W.	A	7
Crutcher, B. F.	E	10
Combs, Jesse	K	10
Cook, John Y.	C	10
Combs, Isaac	C	10 Cav.
Collers, J. B.	A	10
Cannon, W. A.	D	10
Drinkard, F. H.	D	2
Duckmeth, J. S., or		
Dutchworth.	D	14 Cav.
David, W. M.	B	8 "
Dougherty, J.	G	7 "
Deare, Joy A.	E	7 "
Davis, William	C	6 "
Denham, W. F.	H	6 "
Drennan, H.	E	2
Dauthill, J. G.	A	10 Cav.
Dotson, Thomas	A	10
Dodger, J.		Byrne's Batt'y.
Dickson, John	B	10
Evans, C.	C	2 Cav.
Englevan, S. G.	I	3
Erntcher, B. F.	E	2 Cav.
Edward, A. H.	E	6 "
English, W. F.	K	10 "
Evans, James W.	C	10 "
Flannery, D.	E	2 "
Flinn, J. W.	C	7 "
Francis, Simon	A	10
Freeman, James	A	7
Frost, S. W.	B	7 Cav.
Fortner, J. H.	B	5
Falkner, Francis M.	A	1
Floyd, James B.	H	10
Fortner, R. J.	...	2
Fielding S. F.	G	2
Goodman, W. H.	E	2
Greer, W. B., or Green.	A	3

Name.	Co.	Reg't.
Genold, A.	A	3
Gunn, F. A.	E	6
Gassway, S.	G	2
Gawsey, J. F.	G	2
Griggs W. D.	B	2
Gillgen, J. D.	I	8
Gunthery, H., or Gun-		
ther	D	6
Good, G. M.	H	3 Cav.
Gossage, William	I	6
Gavilan, Morris, or		
Gulliam		Byrne's Batt'y
Grady, W. E.	G	6 Cav.
Gallop, William T.	C	6
Gover, S. H.	H	6
Gordan, J. P.	B	8
George, Fred.	K	3
Hedges, James	K	6
Henry, James	K	6
Horne, H.	A	2
Hughes, B. F.	E	8
Hunter, J. G.	D	14 Cav.
Hubbard, C. W.	G	3 "
Huthinson, W. H.	A	6 "
Hifner, H. W.	B	8 "
Hamilton, W.	H	8 "
Harris, J. F.	C	8 "
Hunter, J.	K	10 "
Hensley, James	A	5 "
Hanna, James D.	D	6 "
Hamilton, Thomas	F	7
Hogan, J. D.	G	3
Hinton, B.	E	5
Hutchins, John, shot		
in prison	I	3
Hughes, James A.	I	2
Hughes, W. E.	E	7
Huthins, William H.	B	10
Harrison, S. M.	B	5
Honey, Jesse H.	C	5
Hedges, A.	I	6
Hill, John	B	7 Cav.
Hughes, S. H. or James		
H.	K	6
Holman, J. B.	H	2 Cav.
Hinton, Joseph.	A	5 "
Highley, ——	A	7 "
Hurst, Robert	B	7 "
Henderson, A. C.	F	5 "
Hall, Jason	E	14
Harden, T. W.	D	14
Hanna, J. D.	C	8 Cav.
Harris, W. B.	K	10
Hannan, J. H.	C	2
Hendron, A. C.	F	5
Hughett, Robert B.	C	2
Haney, J. A.	F	10
Huthins, W. C.	G	10
Hinton, R.	E	8
Hill, Robert	...	...
Hedges, H.	K	6
Inglis, W. F.	K	10
Jett, D. A.	D	4
Jordan, J. R.	E	6
Jones, J. W.	C	2 Cav.

Name.	Co.	Reg't.
Jones, John N	B	2 Cav.
Jewel, George W	H	2
Johnson, E. D	A	8 Cav.
Jeff, N. W	A	5 "
Justice, J. P	K	2 "
Jordan, J. W	A	3 "
Jewell, John A	B	2
Johnson, Preston	C	10
Jones, John W	L	2
Knight, D. M	K	10 Cav.
Kuts, G	A	5 "
Keesee, Joseph	D	8 "
Kennedy, H. F		Hanley Batt'y.
Klaners, A. T	B	14
Knox, Robert	C	7 Cav.
King, James W	B	11
Koff, James N. W	D	3
Keen, S. E	B	3
Keller, J. C	D	7
Lusk, H	I	10 Cav.
Langham, H. J	K	8 "
Lucketts, Joseph H	B	10 "
Lloyd, W. B	D	8 "
Landrum, W	G	3 "
Lane, C	A	14 "
Long, James	C	Clark's Cav
Loyall, S	H	10
Lewis, Wm	G	7
Lisk, M. M	I	10
Minhar, T	A or H	1 Cav.
McClure, G. B	B	8 "
Malloy, J. R	D	3 "
Middleton, A. M	C	8 "
Mullins, J. H	A	7 "
Mitchell, Zion	B	17 "
Marshall, A	C	6
Madlen, A. J	A	10
McDaniel, G. W	E	7
McIntosh, James A	D	2
Millard, James	B	10
McCoy, J. H	A	10
Morris, J. C	H	2
Miller, William W	E	6
Morehead, J. R		14
Mitchell, E	A or H	10 Cav.
Martin, T	E	10
Morgan, J. H	B	1 Cav.
Madan, G. W	A	10
Mullis, Joseph	H	10
Mattox, G T	G	7 Cav.
McGuin, M., or McQuinn	D	14
McDaniel, G. W	G	2 Cav.
Mullin, William	G	2 "
Martin, Jesse W	G	2 "
Mifford, A. J	A	10
Malaki, Fred	B	3
Morris, James T	L	2
McCann, Robert		4
Meador, W. H	E	10
Morris, E	C	2
Malley, T. B	D	3
McQuithey, D. M	A	3
Martin, H	E	10
Mitchell, G	B	1
Mullins, James	H	10
Neswick, T. W	D	6 Cav.
Nevitt, J. W	K	8 "
Norman, S	A	7
Noonan, James K	F	7 Cav.
Osborn, R. R	K	6
O'Connor, D. or Jas. D	D	2 Cav.
Oldham, D H	I	10
Owens, James H	A	6
Oaks, C. J		Morgan's Cav.
Patterson, J. R	G	6
Perry, J	B	5
Penn, J. R	E	5
Pattet, Nathan	B	8
Paull, John	A	14
Porter, G. W	C	8 Cav.
Peak, E. C	D	5
Polysarer, W	F	1
Pence, G. W	C	6 Cav.
Pullen, John	C	10
Pedew, B. R	L	2
Quilty, D. M	A	3
Reaves, J. A	H	2
Rogers, M. B	D	3 Cav.
Robinson, A. J	B	3
Richardson, F. F	E	6
Royle, W. H	C	10 Cav.
Richardson, Lee	A	3 "
Rumsey, C	F	5
Roberts, John	C	6
Ring, James W	G	3
Rice, W. G	I	12
Rigney, Henry	H	7
Rice, S H	D	3
Richardson, L	A	2
Smith, William	A	2
Sprons, W. J. M	C	7
Sweeney, J. H	H	6
Smith, Thomas	A	2
Sharp, M	A	8 Cav.
Slusher, J	F	10
Sweeney, S. C	B	8
Story, Zack S. or Strong		Brewer's Co.
Scherley, J. B	B	3
Sullivan, J	G	3
Scearce, G. E	C	3
Spears, Chris	B	8
Summers, W	B	10
Shannon, E. T	E	6 Cav.
Sames, R. W	C	3 "
Smith, Samuel	C	8 "
Starkes, J	B	3 "
Spreve, W. W	E	6 "
Stacy, W. H., or Stazey	B	3 "
Shearer, Robert	B	7 "
Simpson, Rezin	A	7 "
Smith, J. D	D	8 "
Scott, G. B	K	10
Shannon, J. H	E	6 Cav.
Stalling, John	K	8 "
Sweeney, John	C	14
Scrogins, R. E., stabbed	A	5 Cav.
Saunders, John C	C	14
Silvers, T. J	H	6
Setter, John H	C	5

Name.	Co.	Reg't.	Name.	Co.	Reg't.
Shore, Joseph N	G	2	Thompson, D	E	6
Smith, A. B	F	5	Van Buren, B	B	7 Cav.
Sherman, Parker N	C	10	Vaught, T. J	I	2 "
Seaves, Edward	G	8	Vieding, O. H	D	13
Smith, T. C	...	5	Vinden, W	F	2
Sullivan, John	D	5	Watkins, B........G or A	14	
Scott, James A......Martin's	10		Wright, I	H	8 Cav.
Shadwell, W. B	G	3	Watham, W. A	F	10 "
Thomas, J. R	..	8 Cav.	Wicks, G	I	10 "
Traviss, J	A	10 "	Williams, B. J	H	3 "
Tands, J. W	A	7 "	Walker, D. C	K	8
Thompson, J. S	A	6 "	Wickoff, J. M	B	3
Toppas, George	Cobbett's Co., Duke's 2 Reg.		Winn, James M	E	2 Cav.
			Waskem, James	C	10
Turk, Nimrod B	I	2 Cav.	Wade, John	H	7
Thomas, Moses	B	1	Wilson, J. C	B	7 Cav.
Tupman, W. T	I	2	West, W	K	2 "
Tabben, John, or Tot-			Watts, Joseph	F	7
tiu	Byrne's Batt'y.		Woodcock, William	C	7 Cav.
Tracy, Obadiah	C	7	Wasen, W. T	A	14
Thomas, Milton B	K	6 Cav.	Wren, S. E	B	3 Cav.
Terrill, A E	B	7	Whittington, J. B	A	5
Turpin, Emerson	H	7	Wright, Allen	C	2
Tyler, W. H	A	5	Wood, James	G	7
Trendling, S. F	G	2	Williams, James W	E	5 Cav.
Talbert, P. W	B	17	Whir, Henry	G	8 "
Talbert, James	...	2	Winn, P. T	K	8
Tucker, N. B	I	2	Yates, J. C	I	2
Threadwell, D. C	C	6	Young, Odd S	D	14

MISSISSIPPI.

Aggregate dead **446**, classified as follows:

INFANTRY.

From	1st Regiment	14
"	2d "	3
"	3d "	103
"	4th "	29
"	5th "	8
"	6th "	6
"	7th "	7
"	8th "	4
"	9th "	3
"	10th "	2
"	11th "	1
"	12th "	2
"	14th "	64
"	15th "	1
"	16th "	1
"	17th "	3
"	18th "	2
"	20th "	40
"	22d "	5
"	23d "	7
"	24th "	10
"	25th "	4
"	26th "	2
"	27th "	5
"	28th "	3
"	29th "	4
"	30th "	7
"	31st "	1
"	33d "	6
"	34th "	1

INFANTRY.

From	35th Regiment	10
"	36th "	5
"	37th "	18
"	39th "	13
"	40th "	6
"	41st "	2
"	43d "	8
"	44th "	1
"	45th "	10
"	46th "	2
"	50th "	1
"	54th "	1
"	55th "	2
"	57th "	1
"	Mississippi Regiment	2
Citizen		1

CAVALRY.

From	Adams' Regiment	4
"	1st "	1
"	4th "	1

ARTILLERY.

From	Vicksburg Battery	1
"	Adams' "	3
"	Dude's "	1
"	1st "	1
"	3d "	1
"	7th "	2

DETAILS.

Name.	Co.	Regt.
Anderson, J. W.	K	14
Ainsworth, S.	G	37
Abraham, M.	B	45
Aubrey, W.	I	3
Addison, E. W.		Citizen.
Ayres, W. T.	D	3
Alston, W. W.	G	14
Armstrong, A.	F	57
Allison, Isaac.	K	4 Rifles.
Burrows, T.	E	37
Burton, Thomas	H	35
Blackudder, William	H	18
Bloomfield, Geo. H.	I	5
Bridges, H. O.	D	5

Name.	Co.	Reg't.
Bailey, William H.	B	22
Banksteine, O. P.	B	37
Bishop, James.	A	6
Brownlow, I. W.	C	5
Berryhill, M. N.	K	9
Buckley, Thomas.	T	39
Bird, C. M.	E	45
Bailey, E. M.	F	20
Briggs, William	D	3
Brown, J.	I	14
Blair, J.	I	14
Beard, W. H.	A	3
Barnett, J. H.	C	3
Bridges, H. M.	I	3

Name.	Co.	Reg't.
Bradbury, W. D.	D	3
Bargett, Stephen	D	3
Bellair, J. F.	E	1
Bridges, E. H.	E	3
Burke, William	K	20
Blair, John N.	F	14
Barnett, J. W.	C	3
Briggs, G. H.	D	3
Beard, Aleck	Vicksb'g Bat.	
Browncry, D. C.	H	4
Cottrell, James	H	14
Carr, V. D.	C	37
Cotton, John W.	F	1
Cowman, John H.	D	41
Coats, 1. N.	F	7
Cambell, Wm. A.	I Adams' Cav.	
Costlow, George	B	37
Collains, Robert	H	35
Corneaga, Seth	B	24
Corder, E. B.	G	45
Clayton, William	G	14
Cox, F. L. R.	E	2
Cooper, D. J.	E	3
Carroll, John	E	4
Carter, J. S.	A	35
Chambers, G. W.	F	20
Cambell, J R.	A	4
Conners, John	A	3
Coludett, E.	E	20
Creed, R.	H	14
Coulley, M. C.	G	3
Coakies, John	A	21
Coleby, James	G	3
Couch, George	H	1
Cotral, J. A.	G	14
Clecl, R.	H	4
Cook, J.	A	21
Dirke, H.	K	45
Dean, E. W.	E	5
Davies, Albert	I	8
Douglas, Henry	D	7
Deloach, W. D.	D	3
Davis, T. E.	E	3
Daly, B. F.	C	3
Duncan, E. P.	K	14
Dorsey, L. C.	F	10
Dunlap, S.	J	3
Dasey, S.	H	14
Derdes, N. J.	I	3
Derrick, A. F.	G	14
Davis, W.	A	26
Doley, R. T.	C	3
Dardon, N. J.	I	3
Dasey, Thomas	H	14
Duncan, C. B.	K	14
Evans, David	B	35
Elley, Lewis	E	35
Ellcott, M	B	3
Evans, William I.	G	33
Evans, S.	H	13
Edwards, Isaac W.	I	28
Eastward, William	D	3 Batt'y.
Elliot, W. S.	B	20
Elkins, A. J.	A	14
Evan, B. F.	A	14

Name.	Co.	Reg't.
Evans, J. R.	D	3
Esbes, P. B. M.	F	14
Farmer, John P.	L	21
Franklin, C.	I	40
Ferguson, I. I.	H	4
Finley, I R.	C	31
Franklin, C. W.	K	22
Ford, William T.		45
Fitch, John	F	25
Flemming, A.	D	4
Flowers, Milton	K	15
Ford, J. M.	E	3
Fletcher, J. M.	C	3
Fabb, Louis B.	G	14
Fletcher, G. W.	C	3
Flanagan, A S.	B	39
Guess, A. D.	D	37
Gibson, William	G	27
Ganes, James	H	36
Gray, J H.	H	25
Gregory, John C.	I	1
Guiney, Henry M.	K	4
Glenn, W. W.	A	5
Green, A. H.	H	4
Griffon, D.	B	36
Gill, Daniel	B	39
Green, John	C	35
Gooding, Cornelius.	H	4
Gibson, Eli.	K	37
Green, A. B.	B	12
Garbey, J. H.	E	4
Gobb, T. B.	A	20
Green, J.	A	3
Gray, George	F	20
Gentry, J. B.	G	26
Gebanks, F. M.	E	3
Gattus, J H., or Gathin	C	3
Green, E. W.	B	50
Goff, Thomas P.	A	20
Green, George J.	A	3
Gibbon, S B.	C	1
Gillespie, W.	Adams' Cav.	
Hamilton, J P.	C	20
Harlin, T. J.	C	20
Hisaw, James R.	F	14
Hoyle, D L.	I	3
Harris, W. T.	F	25
Houckins, G. H.	Adams' Art'y.	
Haymaker, David	K	43
Hims, William	H	12
Hagenwood, D. M.	I	40
Hannah, James	H	6
Huskinson, James	C	36
Harris, W. I.	F	5
Holbrook, Austin P.	K	44
Harrison, Calorn	Miss. Battery.	
Haygood, I. A.	C	7
Harris, Robert	I	33
Houston, I. L.	G	17
Hipp, Rufus W.	K	22
Hobson, S. R.	F	40
Hathaway, Cain	F	40
Howell, H. I.	K	22
Hayes, I. A.	A	14
Hillaird, O. F.	H	37

Name.	Co.	Reg't.
Holland, A. F.	K	30
Horton, A I.	I	33
Herring, Louis.	G	30
Humphries, J. A.	H	21
Herring, M. D.	D	35
Harding, D.	K	30
Hicks, R.	B	4
House, Nichols.	A	27
Hinton, J. H.	A	17
Harrison, S.	B	4
Hargrave, J. R.	B	3
Hutcher, J. B.	G	3
Hisaw, J. R.	F	14
Hitt, G. W.	I	3
Hopper, J. H.	G	3
Hooved, B C., or Hoover	K	29
Harrison, W. J.	B	4
Holmes, R. M.	J	24
Hhenittau, J. P.	C	20
Harrison, W. J.	B	4
Hamon, J. W.	G	11
Hardy, John.	D	14
Hardin, J. R.	A	3
Henderson, J. C.	G	14
Hethcock, J. R. C.	H	3
Harlies, T. J.	C	20
Holley, H. T.	C	3
Hammett, George.	B	3
Herndon, T. W.	A	20
Hagleman, Robert.	D	20
Hatcher, W. P.	G	3
Hamm, J W	G	14
Isher, E. C.	A	7 Batt'y.
Johnson, John.		1st Miss. Bat.
Jones, A. H.	I	5
Johnson. H. S.	C	37
Johnson, J. E.	K	8
Jones, T. S.		E Miss. Reg.
Jennings, Robert M.	G	4
Jackson, J. C.	A	1
Jackson, J.	H	20
Johnson, S. L.	C or I	3
Jones, A. R.	A	30
Jacues, N. F.	A	3
James, A. F.	A	3
Johnson, William.	A	14
Jones, N. T.	A	3
Johnston. S. J.	I	3
James, B. F.	A	3
Jones, W. R.	A	30
Kater, Joseph M.	E	1
Kimberly, James L.	K	30
Kelly, S. C.	E	14
Kelley, A. S.	F	14
Kent, J. W.	A	3
Kintcannou, D. N.	F	25
Khron, L. H.	E	20
Kenny, J. M.	E	14
Little, Samuel.	G	6
Lewis, Yoe.	I	20
Long, R P.	B	37
Lee, William B. C.	B	37
Lyons, W. A.	F	7
Lewis, John.	K	24

Name.	Co.	Reg't.
Leatherwood, J. C.	B	3
Leester, W.		4
Lawson, J. G.	D	3
Leader, Robert.	D	11
Lindsay, William.	A	23
Lane, H J.	I	14
Leister, W. K.	A	4
Linsing, William.	A	23
Montgomery, A. B.	B	24
Mayes, W. F.	C	4 Cav.
Martin, W. K.	B	28
Murray, T. T.	A	39
Myers, C.	B	6
McKnine, B. F.	D	43
Mare, William A.	G	4
Masgrow, S. B.	G	40
Mohon, Joel.	D	24
Mays, John I.	A	14
Miller, R.	F	39
Murphy, Thomas.	H	28
McRay, James C.	I	11
Marshall, John G.	F	14
McCord, C. R.	F	4
McGraw, J. N.	I	3
Maldwin, John.	B	4
Marble, T. J.	A	30
Moon, J. R.	H	18
McConnell, J. F.	B	20
McKown, J.	A	3
Maldwin, John.	B	45
McGowan, J. M.	A	20
McEsks, F. B.	F	14
McCarthy, J. G.	E	3
Medlon, J J.	B	3
Moncrief, Bishop.	F	14
Moore, Olin.	H	4
McKinney, J.	E	14
Mance, C. M.	G	3
Mills, W. H.	H	20
Miller, J. S.	H	14
Morris, W. W.	I	20
Mitchell, G. M.	B	3
Mitchell, J. M.	B	3
Medlock, N. B.	K	14
Miles, W. H.	H	20
Mapey, E. H.	E	45
Mandwin, John.	B	14
McIlhaney, J. H.	H	46
Mackin, Thomas E.	B	24
Newman, R. W.	K	35
Nabers, M.	F	4
Norton, L. I.	I	35
Norris, Y. L.	B	23
Norgood, I. W.	D	43
Newell, D. A.	I	37
Nichols, Giles.	D	8
Nance, J. H.	G	4
Neal, James H.	H	20
Nicholson, William.	A	10
Nance, C. M.	G	3
O'Neil. John.	E	20
Orwell, Benjamin.	E	3
O'Neil, James A.	H	20
Page, Joseph F.	K	23
Presley, John M.	C	6

Name.	Co.	Reg't.
Parks, Henry C	F	17
Powell, William C	K	14
Pearson, I. A	A	23
Pigg, G. W	H	40
Patterson, R. H	D	41
Patrick, John M	C	37
Pendegrast, Newton	C	27
Pool, James	I	37
Purcel, S. A	A	4
Poe, B. S	G	33
Pollock, William	A	3
Pate, A	A	3
Petty, S	E	3
Pierris, James	A	43
Peters, W. A	G	14
Powell, A	H	3
Pitney, G. M	H	3
Putnam, A. J	F	20
Parks, J. M	G	14
Petty, James	E	3
Ponnell, Alanro	H	3
Pitney, F. M	H	3
Powell, T. J	E	20
Putnam, A. G	I	20
Page, G. W		Dude's Batt'y.
Powell, W. R. B		White's Co., 1st Miss.
Pirie, James	A	3
Page, L. W		Miss. Reg't.
Reynolds, George F	D	3
Roanan, John P	C	37
Renich, Edwin	B	6
Rice, Bryant C	A	3
Robinson, G. W	K	43
Roberts, Thomas	A	4
Reynolds, John	K	2
Rerecine, F. F	F	45
Rushing, S. C	E	33
Robb, R	F	43
Rogers, A	C	39
Ring, A. J	E	39
Ritter, E J	C	3
Robertson, J. P	F	20
Roach, J. H	H	3
Ralph, C. M	C	3
Ragan, J. W	C	3
Reed, J. H	B	3
Rice, P. G	G	14
Rowell, H. B	G	3
Roberts, D. K	H	20
Richardson, R. M	E	3
Ritter, W. H	C	3
Rhodes, T. J		3
Ray, T. J	C	3
Randolph, John L	B	14
Riggin, W. W	C	3
Rice, T. J	G	14
Ralph, J. M	C	3
Rose, S. S		Adams' Art.
Ross, S. S	"	"
Swane, C F	K	22
Simpson, Wesley	A	7
Smith, William A	D	23
Spurlock, Allen	C	39
Smith, James	G	14

Name.	Co.	Reg't.
Sanders, G. W	K	5
Sutter, W. W	A	46
Stokes, John	F	Cavalry.
Simpkins, Monroe		29
Stanton, I. B. H	H	Cavalry.
Shearon, H. G	B	43
Saxton, A	D	14
Spencer, William	B	15
Spears, B. F	B	14
Seeley, G. M	B	20
Shoemaker, G. W	F	35
Snowden, E. R	G	9
Smith, A W	A	39
Snowden, J. G	G	9
Stafford, Edward	H	14
Sealey, G. R. (shot by guard)	B	20
Shaw, J. D	C	20
Smith, A. M	D	3
Smith, James	H	20
Snoued, Samuel	H	3
Schrone, L. H	E	20
Saunders, W. J	D	16
Squires, F. S	D	3
Sweeny, William B	E	14
Smeed, M	C	27
Spears, D. H	H	14
Straught, G. W	B	14
Street, J. F	A	3
Stranlin, G. W	B	14
Sharp, J. F	H	3
Smith, Alfred M	A	3
Symmes, Peyton	D	3
Thomos, Mason M	H	54
Taylor, I. A	E	36
Timms, Jackson	K	37
Treneher, Oliver	C	1 Cav.
Treflord, H	B	55
Thompson, H. L	C	3
Teeman, J. W	B	20
Tomkins, S. B	H	20
Tapp, L. B	G	14
Tuttle, S H	H	4
Taylor, J. A	C	34
Taylor, J. R	E	29
Unknown	A	3
Unknown	D	2
Valentine, I	F	7
Vesper, J. C	B	55
Vance, C. M	G	3
Vance, J. H	G	3
Valentine, N. S	F	1
West, F. G	G	23
Whittington, W. H	G	37
Woods, Henry	G	1
Wells, Jesse	F	7
Williamson, Richard	B	35
Williams, I. H	D	3
Watkins, P. S	D	1
Walters, William	K	8
West, J. B	B	3
Warderly, B	H	14
Watson, D. L	D	4
Wickop, D	A	3
Welsh, R. J	C	1

Name.	Co.	Reg't.	Name.	Co.	Reg't.
West, J. D	G	45	Whitfield, N.M.or N.A.	E	14
Willbrauk, M. A	C	3	Williams, C S	K	14
Wattieccore, J. H	A	14	Watson, C. W	A	3
Woodward, E. E	H	27	Webster, D. K	A	20
Wallace, N	G	3	Williams, O. P	K	14
Webster, A. R	A	20	Winfield, H. H	C	1
Whitter, J. S	H	3	Wilbanks, M. A	C	3
Wetherall, J. A	G	14	Whattimore, J. H	A	14
Wellington, Edward	B	14	Wadington, B	H	14
Watson, H. M	D	3	Yelverton, William B.	K	37
Woodward, T. W. J	A	14	Yerby, J. H	E	4
Winfield, W. H	C	1	Zand, D. A	H	36
Watson, G. W	A	3	Zollicoffer, J. L	K	20

NORTH CAROLINA.

Aggregate dead **397**, classified as follows:

INFANTRY.

From 1st	Regiment		2
" 4th	"		1
" 5th	"		2
" 6th	"		2
" 11th	"		1
" 13th	"		2
" 14th	"		4
" 16th	"		2
" 24th	"		1
" 27th	"		1
" 29th	"		12
" 38th	"		2

INFANTRY.

From 39th	Regiment		1
" 42d	"		1
" 44th	"		1
" 52d	"		5
" 55th	"		1
" 58th	"		9
" 60th	"		13
" 62d	"		210
" 64th	"		78
" 66th	"		1
Reserves			43
Unknown			2

DETAILS.

Name.	Co.	Reg't.	Name.	Co.	Reg't.
Almon, G. G.	D	62	Buchannan, L. C.	H	64
Andrews, S. E.	Reserves.		Bedford, T. G.	K	29
Adams, J.	Reserves.		Bryan, J. M.	B	62
Atkins, J.	B	38	Buckner, Noah	G	64
Atkinson, H. L.	Reserves.		Boston, Jesse	D	62
Anderson, John	F	64	Buchannan, J. W.	H	62
Allen, R. H.	B	64	Butsman, W.	A	62
Anderson, M.	F	64	Bryson, S. G.	H	62
Allison, J. C.	E	62	Bone, John	E	64
Arrington, A.	G	62	Bagrell, A.	Reserves.	
Ash, Ames	H	62	Brown, E. A.	G	62
Adams, James	Reserves.		Bozed, Henry	B	64
Allen, William	A	62	Brown, G. A.	Reserves.	
Ash, Marcus L.	H	16	Bryson, Milton H.	H	62
Allen, B. C.	A	29	Brookcher, John C.	C	29
Anderson, William	F	64	Briggs, John	B	5
Arrington, William P.	G	62	Boggers, M. F.	B	62
Averitt, E. B.	F	62	Baker, William	E	Reserves.
Austin, S. W.	F	62	Brandell, M. D.	D	64
Basny, D. B.	D	60	Bondley, Joseph	E	64
Beddingfeld, C. B.	B	64	Boyle, William S.	Reserves.	
Brown, W. J.	A	64	Boay, Benlin	D	62
Blain, W.	D	62	Barr, H. D.	Reserves.	
Brooks, D.	C	64	Bryant, J. C.	K	62
Bryan, S.	H	62	Brooks, George	C	64
Buckner, J. H.	G	64	Bryant, J. R.	D	64
Blanton, G. N.	H	62	Benjamin, William	A	62
Barnett, J.	B	64	Barnard, J. R.	D	64
Bates, L. M.	D	62	Banning, R. P.	D	60
Brown, Alonzo L.	C	62	Carpenter, A. J.	A	62
Buckner, Eland	D	64	Carson, J. T.	G	62

Name.	Co.	Reg't.
Cadden, H	I	64
Chasplain, Ed	C	62
Crackanar, W	I	64
Conly, Justice	F	58
Caldwell, C. or G	C	62
Cloud, J. E	E	14
Craws, Samuel C	C	62
Coward, J. H	G	62
Chalcl, A. J	K	62
Corr, A. P	B	62
Cornwell, J. B	B	64
Castine, C	K	62
Cochran, James	I	64
Carpenter, Levi	C	11
Crowder, L. M	D	64
Click, William	I	64
Cockerham, H		Reserves.
Chappel, A. J	K	62
Carpenter, B	B	62
Caulip, William B	F	29
Charton, E. C		62
Champbell, Thomas	D	64
Clarke, J. A	D	62
Cline, T. C	D	64
Cate, L. B	B	62
Cook, James G	K	64
Crawford, S. C	G	62
Cash, D	K	62
Dotson, T	A	62
Daniels, H. T	F	64
Danwell, D	B	62
Deuland, C. M	A	60
Dalton, A. J	F	62
Dunlap, W	I	64
Davenport, S. S	B	62
Davenport, C. H	B	62
Dalton, N. W	F	62
Dalton, J. C	F	62
Detts, A. M., or Dietze.	H	62
Dodson, J. A	A	62
Dills, A. J	H	62
Duck, J. W	F	62
Davis, Mathew		Reserves.
Elliot, A. L	F	62
Epley, W. N	F	62
Evans, J. H	I	64
Elleck, W	I	64
Elder, Smith	G	64
Edmonds, Robert	D	64
Eldridge, John		Reserves.
Edney, John C	E	6
Eingham, Job	B	62
Eldridge, M		Reserves.
Flinn, W. H	F	62
Freeman, George	F	62
Fisher, Thomas P	B	14
Frundaw, J. C	D	62
Framell, C	K	62
Finch, John E., or Fincher	C	62
Fate, John	C	62
Ferguson, Robert	A	62
Farnsworth, John W.	I	64
Frances, John W	I	62
Fox, Ambros	A	Reserves.

Name.	Co.	Reg't.
Frauklin, Decatur	I	62
Flood, H. F	A	62
Fowler, E. L	H	62
Gumer, L		Reserves.
Green, Wilson	F	62
Gobush, L. M	I	64
Gurrell, J	F	62
Green, Robert	K	64
Gregg, D	E	55
Gray, John Y	D	62
Galaway, R. M	B	62
Grant, William E	B	62
Guillings, B. M., or Gulliams	H	62
Gisel, Miller	F	6
Goldsmith, William	A	64
Gribbelle, C. or J	D	62
Garton, W. H. H	I	62
Greenley, or Greenlee, A	I	64
Gragg, Samuel	E	58
Griffey, Owen	F	64
Gunter, W. I	H	62
Griffin, A. J. or A. E		
Gunter, S. H	G	62
Gaultney, W. H	H	13
Ganaway, Isham	D	64
Gutzell, J	F	62
Helter, P		Reserves.
Hill, W. A	F	62
Hill, D		Reserves.
Howell, J. M	A	62
Hansan, S. P	I	62
Helston, J	K	64
Hannah, Harry	A	62
Hill, B. F	F	62
Hill, G. W	F	62
Hopkins, John	D	62
Hill, John A	F	62
Hatherly, T	B	64
Hetherby, A. J	B	64
Hooper, Thomas	G	62
Huffman, R. C	C	14
Hellary, J	D	64
Holloway, James	H	62
Hyder, A. K	F	62
Hill, J. B	F	62
Halford, W. P	F	62
Heatherby, Solomon	E	62
Howell, D. S. or D. C.	I	62
Hancock, Jas. or Jos	K	62
Harris, R. W	B	1
Holcomb, J	E	64
Haney, J. A	C	62
Hevner, J. F	B	5
Hetherly, S	B	64
Herren, C	H	62
Hooper, William P	G	64
Hinson, A. M	I	62
Hue, B. J	A	62
Hass, J	E	58
Hudson, Henry		Reserves.
Hondron, William N		Reserves.
Ham, Fred		Reserves.
Hemphill, W. H	I	62

Name.	Co.	Reg't.
Heathley, Solomon	B	62
Hawkins, E	G	62
Hubbard, William N.	Reserves.	
Hann, James	E	62
Hendrean, S. E	Reserves.	
Hollis, Peter	Reserves.	
Hetherly, G. W	E	62
Inman, J	I	62
Inman, D. S	I	62
Iley, W. G	D	62
Irringstone, J	I	62
Jones, H. N	B	62
Jonsen, John	B	64
Johnson, A. W	G	62
Jones, Alfred N	B	62
Jefferson, Atkins	C	58
Jones, Stephen	D	62
Justice, H. W	A	62
Jones, Thomas	B	62
Kay, J	A	62
Keater, J. C	F	62
Keeter, D. A	F	62
King, William	A	29
Ladey, N	Reserves.	
Langst, J. W	I	52
Leguet, W. H	Reserves.	
Long, J. F	I	62
Lucado, J. W	F or H	62
Lance, William D	D	60
Lenning, John	C	62
Long, E. W	F	62
Longford, J. M	D	64
Larley, John F	I	62
Lane, William	D	60
Lewis, William	K	60
McCracken, D. S	A	62
Morrow, J	F	58
Messar, D	C	62
Mooney, G	A	62
Mell, R	I	62
Matin, A	F	64
Mathews, W. D	B	62
Mountoulk, George	H	60
McConnel, E. W	B	39
McCabe, L. B	B	62
Mason, P	I	62
Morgan, L	D	64
Molton, J. W	F	62
Morgan, J. E	B	64
Moore, M	C	62
McCloud, J. H	D	62
McGuinnis, James	F	62
McElroy, Jas. or Jos.	C	62
McCall, F. T	E	64
Mayhaffney, J. S	C	62
Morton, H. S	D	62
Myers, John	H	62
Morgan, Alfred	B	64
McClure, W. B	A	62
Mann, Jesse	C	27
McCall, Charles	E	62
McTaggard, David	B	62
Mason, John	I	62
Morrison, Joseph	A	29
McCabe, Thomas J	C	62
Moran, John	F	58
McLow, James H	D	62
Manning, —	Reserves.	
Millard, Harmon	B	62
Marion, G	Reserves.	
May, John	F	62
Mantroth, George	H	60
Norton, A. W. or A. M.	A	64
Northrop, Jesse	A	14
Nash, Amos	H	62
Norton, H. L	D	52
Orr, George	E	62
Owens, J. R	E	62
Price, J	A or H	29
Philips, J. W	F	29
Pointtle, J. R	Reserves.	
Parington, W	G	62
Preswell, A. J	C	62
Poor, William	H	61
Pless, A	I	62
Posey, Leo. W. or George W.	K	64
Plott, H. J	A	62
Plott, C. L	H	62
Petersen, E	K	62
Parker, Samuel	E	58
Parker, H. J	B	Reserves.
Paulep, William	C	64
Pickson, Daniel	A	29
Poole, W. D	I	52
Peck, George	A	64
Peters, J. W	Reserves.	
Pendleton, J. R	Reserves.	
Prater, Josiah	D	62
Pater, T. M	C	42
Patterson, E	K	62
Penthram, C. M	A	60
Ruft, S. T. or S. P	A	62
Robertson, J	I	62
Ring, W. D	A	29
Read, James F	Reserves.	
Rykaid, R. H	K	62
Roberts, B	C	64
Reece, James	I	62
Reaves, Avery	E	62
Rateliff, J M	C	62
Rogers, M. C	I	62
Rice, J. W	F	64
Radford, R. F	K	29
Rumsay, J. A	A	64
Robinson, W. M	H	62
Ruth, Wilson	D	60
Reese, J. J	Reserves.	
Rice, W	K	61
Redmond, L. H	K	16
Reynolds, H. C	A	29
Ray, John	A	62
Roan, John R	D	...
Rogers, William		62
Stivers, A	C	4
Strasney, F. M	I	62
Shipman, W. R	B	60
Smartley, C	F	64
Seay, Benjamin	A	62
Sturgeon, S. M	Reserves.	

Name.	Co.	Reg't.
Spencer, E.		Reserves.
Shale, James	A	24
Sellers, Jack	C	62
Shelton, James L.	A	62
Sanger, John	C	64
Spangler, A.	G	11
Searsey, A. H.	F	62
Scragg, Nathan	E	62
Stroup, J. R.	F	60
Simpson, J. B.	E	62
Salmon, W. M.	F	62
Shafford, William	I	64
Sellers, J. M.	B	62
Sentell, J. N.	B	64
Shepard, W.	E	62
Snyder, H. S.	D	62
Sawyers, Thomas F.	G	64
Stepp, William	K	60
Smith, Charles L.	B	62
Smith, Seth		1 Bat'y.
Stuman, James	F	64
Smith, A. C.	B Reserves.
Satchey, Newton		Reserves.
Shipwat, Gilland		Reserves.
Sanders, M.	D	62
Shelton, F. W.	C	52
Sheldon, G. P.	B	62
Smith, William F.	F	52
Stafford, W. M.	G	62
Sawyer, John	E	64
Sloan, G. W.		44
Spethens, A.	C	64
Stauning, F. H.	I	62
Tartan, D. M.	A	62
Turgeson, R.	A	62
Tascott, S.	E	58
Teague, J.	A	62
Tipton, Thomas	A	62
Thompson, J. W.	F	62
Twett, L.	I	62

Name.	Co.	Reg't.
Thompson, B. Y.	D	62
Teague, William		Reserves.
Taylor, James	C	58
Thompson, Silas	F	62
Tuspin, H. A.	C	62
Turner, Lawrence		Reserves.
Tritton, L.	I	62
Wade, George	A	62
Wilson, J.	E	62
Weld, F. or Wills	D	64
Willard, Barney	F	62
Ward, J. E.	A	62
Watson, E.	H	62
Watson, G. H.	G	62
Willings, B. M.	H	62
Wooster, S. S.	I	62
Wallace, Jerry	E	62
Waldron, J. F.	B	64
Williams, James	H	62
Whalen, Archie	F	64
Wood, P. B.		Reserves.
Walker, William	A	64
Webb, L. H.	H	62
Wood, Benjamin	H	62
Willis, T. R.	A	64
Wilborn, Henry	B Reserves.
Woolton, E. B.	C	62
Williams, Thomas W.	B	66
Walker, R. P.	B	38
Whitmire, Andrew J.	K	62
Washburne, Thos. N.	I	62
Watson, James A.	G	62
Wood, G. W.	F	62
Wooten, L. S.	I	62
Wade, Joseph E.	A	62
White, James	F	13
Young, J. A.	G	62
Yoder, C.		Reserves.
Zenning, J. H.	C	62

TENNESSEE.

Aggregate dead **747,** classified as follows:

INFANTRY.

From	1st Regiment	16
"	2d "	11
"	3d "	43
"	4th "	13
"	5th "	5
"	6th "	4
"	7th "	3
"	8th "	25
"	9th "	4
"	10th "	31
"	11th "	3
"	12th "	5
"	13th "	5
"	14th "	4
"	15th "	30
"	16th "	7
"	17th "	12
"	18th "	9
"	19th "	7
"	20th "	3
"	23d "	1
"	24th "	2
"	25th "	6
"	26th "	10
"	27th "	4
"	28th "	3
"	29th "	6
"	30th "	1
"	31st "	4
"	32d "	1
"	34th "	1
"	37th "	2
"	38th "	3
"	40th "	14
"	41st "	1
"	42d "	74
"	43d "	5
"	44th "	3
"	15th "	5
"	16th "	22

INFANTRY.

From	47th Regiment	1
"	48th "	48
"	49th "	60
"	50th "	79
"	51st "	2
"	55th "	46
"	59th "	1
"	60th "	2
"	61st "	3
"	64th "	1
"	Biffel's Regiment	6
"	Taylor's "	1
"	Ward's "	1
"	Crawford's Battalion	2
"	Barnes' "	3
"	Cries' "	1
"	Johnson's Rifles	1
"	Reynolds' "	3
Conscripts		4
A Citizen of Nashville		1

CAVALRY.

From	1st Regiment	6
"	4th "	2
"	8th "	5
"	9th "	1
"	10th "	1
"	18th "	1
"	Cox's Battalion	20
"	Bennet's "	2
"	Orchard's "	1
"	Green's "	1
"	Unknown	1

ARTILLERY.

From	Maury's Battery	9
"	Kane's "	9
"	Raines' "	7
"	Kane's or Raines' Battery	5
"	Newman's "	1
"	Donson's "	1

DETAILS.

Name.	Co.	Reg't	Name.	Co.	Reg't.
Atkinson, William	D	42	Aiken, James M	C	48
Adolett, George	B	3	Arcritt, Richard	G	49
Aslop, William	H	50	Adams, B. B	A	50

Name.	Co.	Reg't.
Aller, G. F.		Maury's Art.
Aiken, H. S.	C	48
Austerhisen, O. R.	D	49
Allen, Newton	I	49
Adams, C. J.	K	50
Alexander, H. W.	I	49
Austin, S. W.		Conscript.
Allen, J. A.	A	Newman's
Allman, J. B.	A	5 [Bat'y.
Albert, Newton		6
Asheroft, William D.	A	10
Austin, John B.	B	16
Armstrong, George D.	C	48
Blanton, George	G	49
Best, James	G	49
Bradshaw, George	G	42
Boswell, Drury	K	3
Bass, J. M.	K	49
Black, J. A.	K	50
Buchanan, R. D. or		
D. B.	I	50
Brown, J. R.	D	49
Batten, A.	G	50
Brooks, W. F.	C	50
Brewer, Solomon	G	42
Bastain, D. L.	I	42
Baughus, R. C. A.	K	48
Burch, B. B.	B	42
Burk, Henry	E	49
Burton, W. P.	A	3
Bumpass, Zebedee	G	49
Bishop, A. L.	B	50
Bradbury, James	G	50
Barrett, Jasper	I	50
Bond, D. M.	A	48
Bearden, Ansel	H	42
Branch, W. P.	B	3
Brooker, William J.	H	50
Bastion, William	I	42
Bryant, D F.	K	50
Bailey, J. H.	E	48
Ball, F. M.	H	48
Brewer, William	D	55
Brewer, Lewis	D	55
Beake, B.	C	40
Briggs, H. C.	F	55
Bailey, Wesley	I	55
Blackenship, J.	C	55
Black, J. M.	D	55
Barnhill, S. A.	B	46
Bane, J. W. or J. M.	K	42
Busby, J.	K	40
Barrem, T. C.	G	50
Birdwell, B.	K	3
Belcher, W. T.	G	15
Byle, H B.	D	15
Black, T. B.	D	15
Bush, G. W.	I	14
Barton, N. J.	B	7
Brown, James H.	F	18
Brown, A. J.	F	8
Bartlett, Joshua A.	K	8 [Reg't.
Boys, James W.	K	Biffel's
Bowlin, Dollis		Reynold's
Brown, W. J.	A	11 [Rifles.

Name.	Co.	Reg't.
Brown, L. B.	G	8
Bocum, William	A	Cox's Bat.
Barham, Thomas	B	Cox's Bat.
Bridge, John R.	D	8
Bond, Jonathan	B	4
Bradford, William	A	10
Bridwell, John	C	19
Black, B (darkey)		Ward's Reg't.
Burdett, J W	B	14
Banty, John		Raines' Bat'y.
Brown, W. B.	G	17
Buckalin, W. G.		Raines' Bat'y.
Brown, Wm		" "
Barker, James K	A	5
Baltriff, Calvin	B	2
Bates, Thomas B.	I	43
Berrins, J	C	45
Black, J. T.	D	15
Breeding, Asa	A	1
Brown, William	B	55
Balch, Joseph O.	A	17
Bruce, E		Conscript.
Blackman, G	C	2
Brewster, J. E.		Cavalry.
Brock, M		Kane's Bat'y
Brooks, W. S.	C	5
Borum, J. S.	D	27
Beyes, James M.		Biffel's Reg't.
Cunningham, Alfred.	G	49
Cochran, Michael.	D	10
Chandler, F. N.	C	42
Clymer, Charles	B	49
Carlick, J. S.	H	26
Cheatham. J. W.	E	3
Chandler, J. M.	I	42
Carter, John	C	50
Caldwell, William	D	26
Condis, J. F.	K	49
Cox, S. H.	I	49
Chandler, R. G.	I	42
Chandler, Shelby	K	48
Cooper, A. M. C.	K	42
Cooper, S. G	H	3
Carson, J. A.	D	46
Cushen. J. P.	C	42
Carter, W. M. E...K or E		1
Cook. P. H.		Maury's Art.
Cloud, R.	H	26
Culley, J. R.	I	49
Clanton, A. C.	C	3
Cinnouel, Daniel	K	10
Cherry, B.	B	55
Cobb, J. G.	G	55
Cardwell, A. E.	D	3
Clifton, B. J. ...B or K		49
Charlton, J K	K	4
Cocke, J. B.	C	15
Cox, James	K	18
Cragg, A. C.	C	55
Cobb, James	B	Biffel's Reg.
Clarke, W. C.	H	8
Cason, J. E.	G	47
Cearley, P. D.	H	27
Coppage, J. V.	B	28
Cochran, C.		Kane's Bat'y.

Name.	Co.	Reg't.
Carpenter, Leroy		Kane's or Raines' Bat'y.
Couch, William H	B	12
Clonnigan, John		Kane's or Raines' Bat'y.
Choates, Samuel	B	15
Cake, James B	C	15
Carter, James C..	C	1
Conevan, Charles P...	G	34
Cope, E	C	48
Canada, H	A	42
Cross, R. B	G	60
Caudwell, W. H	F	15
Carms, W. D	C	43
Carter, William	F	4
Carmon, R	H	31
Ceasley, P. S	I	27
Colbert, J. C	H	9
Coff, S. G	G	55
Cooper, J. S	H	3
Cobbs, James F	K	28
Cochran, C		Kane's Bat'y.
Curby, Robert	E	50
Derryberry, M. E., or Duberry	A	48
Dupee, C. J	F	49
Damele, Ed	G	49
Davenport, W. H	E	49
Dunkard, F. E	B	1
Dockery, J. N		Maury's Art.
Defoe, T. C	I	3
Duffer, J. E	D	55
Duke, W. G	E	48
Dixon, Robert C	F	49
Dowdy, Uriab	I	50
Dagley, J. R		Kane's or Raines' Bat'y.
Davis, A. J	B	Donson's Battery.
Dowell, John	A	Cox's Bat.
Doyle, James	I	18 Cav.
Donaldson, A. J	B	17
Doak, James M., or Deak		Kane's Raines' Bat'y.
Davis, J. P.	C	17
Davidson, John R	I	19
Dalton, John	C	12
Dwyer, John N	E	38
Dowley, John	E	2
Ditze, T. J	L	11
Delano, J	B	15
Davis, William	H	26
Drake, B	C	40
Early, James	I	49
Egan, Anthony	D	10
Easley, Thomas	I	48
English, N. E	A or F	40
Evans, John	F	42
Edwards, G. W	C	17
Erwin, R. L	A	8 Cav.
Ellis, W. J	C	8 -
Estes, James F	I	48
Ezell, Samuel.	B	1
Eggleston, V. J	C	6
Elliot, William..	A	1

Name.	Co.	Reg't.
Edmistor, Joseph M...	F	9
Edwards, James R	B	20
Elliott, C. V	C	20
Fisher, George W		3
Freely, William	B	10
Forrester, S. N	D	48
Fisher, John D	I	3
Fox, Harris	A	48
Frulin, James	D	42
Ford, W. D	B	49
Freelon, James	B	42
Fisher, J. A. C	B	10
Fleming, Charles B...	I	18
Furlond, James C	H	48
Fisher, J. N	A	59
Falkner, Thomas	B	Cox's Bat.
Freeman, T. C	K	1
Fike, R. C	K	40
Freelow, Joseph	D	42
Fauburgh, M. M		Barnes' Bat.
Goodman, C. H	H	3
Goodman, C. B..	C	50
Griggs, G M	G	3
Golden, J. M	E	3
Goodwin, R. J		Maury's Art.
Gilbert, Webster..	A	42
Gormon, William	B	50
Grisham, Solomon	E	46
Gunn, J. M	E	50
Gibbons, Michael	H	42
Gross, M. J	K	42
Graves, D. A	E	48
Glasgow, W. P	I	50
Grant, James	A	Citizen of Nashville.
Gester, Robert	E	50
Goodman, James A	B	48
Gassett, Merwa, or Gossett	B	50
Giaron, Thomas P	D	50
Glazer. T	H	12
Green, T. H	G	46
Garrison, George	A	50
Grinder, J. C	H	3
Grisham, N. M	G	46
Garner, Robert	D	50
Gibson, A. T	C	10
Gross, T	D	8
Gray, W. V	A	8 Cav.
Grison, Lewis A		Biffel's Bat.
Goodrow, J	B	Cox's Bat.
Graham, W. C	H	18 Bat.
Gish, A	I	8
Gray, J. V	I	15
Grove, Presley	D	8
Glenn, John	G	50
Glenn, Robert	B	38
Gibson, G. T	F	2
Garrett, William	A	15
Gravitt, John M	K	1
Gaither, W. B	H	18
Green, E. M..	B	50
Garrison, George	A	55
Guldy, J. B	I	49
Granbough, M. M		Barnes' Bat.

Name.	Co.	Reg't.
Gill, W. O.	B	Crawford's Battery.
Glenn, Samuel J.		Raines' Bat'y.
Henderson, J. B.	H	26
Holt, W. R.	F	49
Harmon, H. H.	K	50
Hackney, Stephens	A	29
Hodges, J. S.	C	48
Harris, William	K	48
Higgs, T. B.	C	49
Howell, G. W.		42
Hull, J. W.	D	50
Hamm, Joseph	B	49
Harris, John	B	50
Hackett. P.	D	10
Helmock, Hiram	C	3
Hogue, W. A.	B	42
Hinson, C. L.	A	43
Harwell, B F.	A	3
Harris, Elias	K	48
Hunt. Joel	E	42
Hensley, James B.	E	42
Hubbell, T. C., or T. S.	D	3
Hogan, J F.	F	42
Harris, J. T.	B	49
Harperson, J H.	D	48
Hudson, Silliman or Gilman	I	50
Henderson, J B.	D	42
Hendricks, S. W.	K	50
Hewett, E.	B	40
Hans, G. L., or Hawse.	B	46
Harvey, W. J.	A	50
Hudson, William R.	A	55
Holden, Elias	B	46
Hunt, Robert	G	55
Hendricks, J. J.	B	50
Hendrix, Charles	D	1
Harris, W. H.	B	50
Harris, Samuel	C	49
Harris, W.	K	49
Holder, James	C	55
Holder, James	E	48
Harris, Thomas	D	42
Harper, J. M.	A	55
Herron, J. D.	A	55
Hutchinson, J. M.	I	42
Hensley, E. D. T.	B	48
Haskins, Robert	A	49
Holmes, J. C.	B	55
Herron, W. W.	A	55
Hogan, E. A.	H	50
Hanby, J. N.	D	2
Haunce, W.	H	12
Hardem, J. E.		61
Harris, W. B.	H	10 Cav.
Hodges, Martin	F or I	3
Hocklin, James B.	H	13
Hall, James B.	A	44
Hotchkiss, R. S.	A	1 Cav.
Hall, Stephen	A	Cox's Bat.
Hooper, D. S.		Bennet's Bat.
Huddleston, George B.	C	8
Holmes, Comada	F	8 Cav.
Heard, E. B.	C	1 "

Name.	Co.	Reg't.
Hopkins, Sterling.B or	D	29
Hudson, W. C.	I	8
Haynes, J. R.	B	Cox's Bat.
Harris, James M.	B	4
Hill, J. G., or Hillis	A	31
Hoster, A. J.	H	1
Holden, Jonathan	G	44
Hughes, Aaron	B	29
Hudson, Thomas B.	A	55
Huddle, James H.		Kane's Batt'y.
Herring, B	C	51
Hopper, James R. P.	C	17
Hagan, William		55
Hayes, William	C	48
Hudgens. William	D	8
Heston, A. J	H	1 Cav.
Hunter, H J		4 "
Hehbode, Noah.	H	10
Hotchkiss, R. S.	I	1
Haines, W. H.	B	50
Hicks, T. R	C	49
Hison, William		9th Battalion.
Hamm, J	B	29
Hendricks, R.	D	50
Harris, J		42
Hall, J. W.	D	5
Harperson, J. S.	D	40
Hogan, J. T	F	43
Holt, W. R.	F	19
Hickey, S.	C	29
Ivey, R. A.	K	3
Irwin, R. L.	A	8
Jordan, W. R.	I	Cox's Bat.
Jennings, C. P.	I	18
Johnson, J. R.	A or H	24
Jones, John	G	10
Jones, S W.	C	50
Jannett, J. R.	F	49
Jackson, H. E.	F	42
Johnson, E. W.	B	3
James, Carter	A	42
Johnson, T. J	C	48
Johnston, E	B	42
Jennison, C. W.	K	40
Jones, S. L.	I	40
Jones, John	B	55
Johnston, S. Y	H	42
Journey, R. F.	F	45
Johnston, W. R.		Maury's Art.
James, Adrian or Adam	H	26
Johnston, E. C.	I	3
Jones, W.	B	55
Jenkins, W W.	I	10
Jennings, Royal.		Conscript.
James, J. C.		Biffel's Reg't.
Jordan, Archer.	I	15
Johnson, R.	F	18
Jackson, James.	I	6
James, R. G.	K	8
Jones, James S	D	48
Jones, R.	B	16
Kean, Michael.	G	49
Kitts, Tilman.	D	26
Kittrell, William A.	C	3

Name.	Co.	Reg't.
Kendrick, Rufus	D	50
Kirby, Robert	E	50
Key, E. C	C	50
King. Robert	C	3
Key, P. L	F	46
Kennedy, J. F	E	50
Kimble, B. F	B	Cox's Bat.
Kallent, J. C	H	19
Key, F. L	E	16
Kenner, Joseph		1 Art.
King, D. A	A	15
Kimball, B. B	B	Cox's Bat.
Legalt, Hugh		Raines' Bat'y.
Lockridge, W. J	G	10
Levering, H. M	D	42
Lourie. A. H	E	46
Leavitt, William	C	10
Lenox, J. C	B	50
Lee, Duncan	K	46
Lucas, J M	B	46
Lowe, Cyrus	1	42
Lessenberry, Robert	E	48
Liston. Robert	E	55
Lisk, Robert	E	55
Lee, Darby	K	10
Lills, W	D	50
Lane, G. W	G	2
Lockwood. E	A	16
Ledger, H. G	E	1 Cav.
Livingston, N	C	Cox's Bat.
Layme, William	B	Cox's Bat.
Lathrop, Robert	G	2
Lauter, Thomas	F	2
Lisk, Daniel C	A	29
Lockhart, William L	H	10
Lane, Thomas	H	64
Lee, S. G	A	19
Moore, W. H	H	48
Morrison, J L	G	49
Martin, J. C	K	42
Milan, A. C., or Miller.	1	50
McCormick. Edward.	H	10
Martin, W. T	G	50
Moore, Robert P	1	50
Moharty, John	I	10
MacIntyre, William	D	42
McTagg, John	G	10
Morrison, A. J	1	42
McLean, William	C	10
Morgan, J. R	A	46
Murphy, J S	E	48
Moody, R	A	50
Martin, B. G	D	49
McDonald, W	E	5
Martin. A. J	B	50
Mark, J M	D	50
Morris, J. M	D	50
Moody, W. J	E	46
Mitton, W. R	B	55
McAllister, James	B	50
McGlathery, W. B	H	42
McMinn, O. P	A	42
Murray, T	B	48
Morrison, T. B	1	42
Mincher, Lewis	D	42

Name.	Co.	Reg't.
Mathers, J. C	E	51
McDaniel, M	A	55
Miller, Horton	D	40
Meenach, R. T	B	40
McDaniel, Thomas	F	42
McCall, J. B	B	49
Morehom, John	K	49
Malone, Benjamin	H	42
Moore, E	F or I	46
Mullenae, Levi, or		
Mullens	D	1
Mann, M. T	D	15
McClure, T. B	C or G	41
McDonald, R. T	G	8
Morgan, Elijah	A	8
Manabank, John, or		
Marchbranch	A	Cox's Bat.
Moore, J. M	G	45
Moore, James	E	8
Moore, William M	D	8
Marr, William	A	8 Cav.
Morrison, D. B	B	Cox's Bat.
Mathews, James	E	37
McNutt. W B		Kane's or Raines' Batt'y.
McClintock, Isaac	A	13
McCoy, George W	E	61
McDaniel, R F	G	3
Monaghan, John	A	43
McMurrog, J. M	A	1
Munday, James		Kane's Bat'y.
McGanty, James	1	15
McDowell, William	G	9
Mayberry, W. W	G	10
Meyers, William R	1	44
McDaniels, H	B	25
Moore, A. H	G	45
Martin, D S	E	37
McLean, William	A	10
Mowers, Thomas H	A	Crawford's
McMasters, J	B	50
Meek, H. M	A	Cries' Bat.
McCarthy, John B.		Barnes' Bat.
Nite, W. H	C	42
Nisler, David	E	55
Newman, Leonard	C	50
Nolan John	F	1
Niblett, S. O	F	42
Nares, J	K	42
Nicholson, W. D	K	49
Norris, John		Conscript.
Nipple, Nelson		Johnson's Rifles.
Nicholes, C. W	A	15
Noyes, Reuben	K	19
Narion, H. D	A	3
Nichoheld, William	H	10
Norris, S. J	K	42
Nichols, J. F	K	48
Orgain, D. B	A	49
Osford, James	B	48
Owens, J. M	B	42
Oliver, W. S	E	17
Oden, G. W	E	17
Omen, W. H	G	13

Name.	Co.	Reg't.	Name.	Co.	Reg't.
O'Neal, J. M	I	15	Randall, J. C	D	42
Oakes, D		Kane's Batt'y.	Rustin, H. R	A	Cox's Bat.
Owens, I. H	I	7	Rogedale, T. M	H	2
Owens, William H	G	15	Radford, J	I	15
Ober, S		Coxs' Bat'n.	Rayner, H. C	A	15
Powers, E. H	E	49	Roarke, R. J	G	15
Powell, N. D	E	49	Ring, David E	A	15
Parrott, James	I	50	Rollin, Benjamin	K	50
Phillips, T. B	H	26	Rolland, Eli	K	48
Potter, John R	C	50	Rose, Joseph P	C	4
Pickard, S. S	C	3	Riley, Richard	A	17
Page, John	C	42	Roberts, Joseph H	F	31
Powell, A. J	E	49	Rippe, A	E	15
Pendegrast, Jason	K	42	Reyland, E. O	F	4
Perkins, W. M	H	26	Ryle, H. B	D	15
Pollock, J. M	B	18	Rigby, William	F	18
Powell, S. O	F	46	Rucker, S M	C	10
Pate, B. M	C	42	Rooker, W. G	H	50
Parker, T. H. or J. H	D	46	Rasson, S. L	I	42
Peuer, G. W	C	48	Smith, E. C	F	49
Pains, J	H	42	Summer, William	F	50
Presson, W. R	A	55	Stevens, Thomas	F	49
Porter, John H	E	50	Sanders, H. M	B	49
Potts, A. R	D	46	Scarborough, John	I	50
Prefford, H	B	55	Snodgrass, G		Maury's Art.
Pugh, M. A	E	48	Stewart, B	"	"
Poteat, Edward J	D	3	Sanders, T. G	I	42
Pope, A. J	H	3	Sellers, O. B	D	42
Page, R. H	D	55	Simms, J. H	F or E	46
Pace, M. J	F	49	Sutton, O. M	I	42
Pool, H	B	46	Svimore, J. W., or Siz-		
Perry, J	I or G	55	amore	D	49
Philips, J. M		Biffel's Reg't.	Sargeant, J. C	H	50
Prater, Isaiah	D	8	Smith, Aaron	F	42
Pope, L. M		B Cox's Bat.	Stringer, John	C	10
Proctor, William..E or	F	11	Sturgess, John	C	10
Pollock, Calvin	D	18	Sparlock, John	E	42
Prior, Dan	E	10	Steward, C. C	D	50
Powmau, J. J	A	25	Street, S. R	H	38
Plumlee, J		Raines' Bat'y.	Smith, A. G	D	55
Pierce, William	D	1	Samply, George	B	42
Potato, Edward I	D	3	Spalding, A. O	B	49
Patton, James R	F	15	Sample, Martin	B	42
Porter, E. B	D	61	Smith, Lewis	I	49
Pullen, R. P	A	23	Smith, S. D	H or C	50
Plumble, Joseph		Kane's Bat'y.	Smith, R	G	55
Perrison, William	F	55	Scott, W. S	D	3
Presson, B. F	A	55	Smith, Nathan	I	49
Philips, H. B	B	26	Smith, L. L	D	48
Powell, T. J	E	10	Smith, G. W	I	49
Porter, John	C	50	Simpson, R. T	A	40
Paine, J. G	G	4	Stanfield, G. W	B	50
Quinlan, James	B	48	Sadler, R. F	I	40
Ross, L. W	D	3	Smith, John	I	10
Robinson, Henry J	A	48	Sullivan, A	I	15
Ruffin, Thomas	C	50	Smith, A. M	C	17
Richardson, James	C	30	Smith, John		Orchard's Cav.
Roberts, W. R	I	10	Simpson, S. T		B Cox's Bat.
Rutledge, J. D	B	3	Simpson, R. L	C	1 Cav.
Robinson, G. W		Maury's Art.	Smith, J. M		Reynolds'
Roundtree, J. R	K	48			Rifles.
Rawlin, T. S	H	55	Stowe, J. M	H	8
Robinson, Thomas	I	50	Summerlin, D	K	6
Renford, W. J	E	48	Senter, A. W	F	13
Richardson, E. J. Y	H	50	Sholes, J. M	D	10

Name.	Co.	Reg't.
Shru, John A	A	15
Sharp, Robert	G	2
(Schone) Schnoter, William H	E	2
Sullivan, Anderson	F	17
Shark, J. F	H	3
Shephard, L. O		3
Scott, J	K	1
Sitts, W	D	50
Sadler, R. T	I	60
Sweeney, Joseph	B	Taylor's.
Scott, T. J	E	3
Sherry, B	B	55
Tuppett, Marion, or Tripett	H	49
Taylor, George	G	50
Thompson, Jas ..A 5 or	A	50
Thompson, James J.	E	3
Talley, S. G	D	7
Tucker, J. R	C	55
Turner, Samuel	H	3
Taylor, J. F	G	49
Telford, G. W	B	49
Tremier, Pizarro	H	42
Thomas, J. S. or J. A..	H	42
Tynor, J	I	49
Tomlinson, W. D	I	50
Turnbour, J	E	48
Taylor, W. W	G	55
Trambrough, W. H	F	42
Talbert, P. W	B	17
Taylor, J. L	H	1 Cav.
Tayne, J. C	G	4
Taugh, S. L	L	13
Theregher, J. W. or Thresher	I	25
Thompson, J. M	A	Green's Cav.
Todd, C. H	D	4 Cav.
Tays, R. W	I	4
Toombs, T		45
Tuckerson, W. B	B	60
Toole, Patrick	B	15
Turner, A. J	D	12
Townsend, J. J	A	25
Taylor, T	F	12
Tisdale, R. H	E	32
Tenderson, C. W	K	40
Thomas, James		Reynolds' Rifles.
Van Hook, James	K	42
Vernon, John	I	42
Vick, Thomas W	I	12
Vick, P. V	D	50
Vesler, J. C	B	55
Vault, J. M	D	55
Vanney, C	G	8 Cav.
Visor, William		9 "
Woods, Henry		Kane's Bat'y.

Name.	Co.	Reg't.
West, William	D	8
Wright, R. H	C	8
Williams, James	B	48
Wilkinson, D. G	F	19
Welsh, W	C	48
Warner, John	I	50
Watson, William	I	49
Weight, J. H	A	48
Waldrop, James H	B	3
Walker, R	D	49
White, W. W	E	3
Willis, G	D	46
Wilkinson, J. G	F	46
Williams, J K. P	K	42
Weakly, W. E	F	42
Weakly, John M	F	42
Willoughby, J. H	C	50
Williams, James	E	49
Walker, James	H	55
Wilson, W	C	55
Winter, R. F	F	48
Wood, J. H	D	42
Wells, J. D	C	50
Williams, J. M...B 42 or	B	46
Webb, J. T	G	55
Whyte, B. F	A	49
Wright, W. H	I	20
Wealthy, W. S	C	16
Wade, W. G		Barnes' or Kane's Bat'y.
Ward, J. M.	D	Bennett's Cavalry.
Webb, George	D	8
Williams, J. M. or J.W.	H	8
Washburne, A H		Cox's Bat.
Williams, R. G.	H	8
Warnell, Richard	A	4
Ward, Richard	A	4
West, J. S	I	15
Woods, Henry		Raines' Batt'y.
Wright, A. L. or A. C..	D	25
Willeford, J. H	I	25
Waueer, James	A	14
Waddrell, H. D	C	1
Warren, Elijah	I	24
Winke, Lazarus	B	48
Webb, Thomas	F	15
Whiley, C. H		I
Westmoreland, R. H..	B	3
Whittaker, D. I	C	27
Whitmell, T		31
Walker, William	I	19
White, William L	A	16
Webb, George H	C	14
Wheally, W. S	D	16
Yorkner, Thomas	B	Cox's Bat.
York, W. P	E	28

TEXAS.

Aggregate dead **608**, classified as follows:

INFANTRY.

From 1st Regiment		4
" 2d "		6
" 3d "		5
" 4th "		1
" 5tb "		1
" 6tb "		1
" 7tb "		72
" 8th "		3
" 9tb "		3
" 10th "		116
" 11tb "		3
" 12tb "		2
" 13th "		2
" 14th "		6
" 15th "		103
" 16th "		2
" 17th "		123

INFANTRY.

From 18th Regiment		124
" 19th "		5
" 23d "		1
" 25th "		1
" 30th "		1
" 32d "		3
" 41st "		1
" 48tb "		1
" 50th "		2
" Taylor's Regiment		1
" Det. Co. Spies		1
Unknown		2

CAVALRY.

From Johnson's		9
" Richard's		2
" 8th Regiment		1

DETAILS.

Name.	Co.	Reg't.	Name.	Co.	Reg't.
Anthony, W. R.	H	2	Botomy, William	H	10
Akins, J. M	I	7	Beard, W.	II	10
Athens, George E.	B	17	Browner, D. S.	D	7
Asheraft, W. D.	A	10	Brown, L. L.	I	10
Ames, Thomas	K	18	Barry, Jos.	II	11
Anderson, John	B	15	Blackman, Wm. C.	Johnson'sCav.	
Abney, N. A	J	17	Browner, J S.	D	7
Anthony, Meredith G.	J	15	Bartlett, Hiram.	C	7
Atwood. R. T.	B	18	Barham, J. C.	G	2
Allen, B. F.	D	18	Brown, C. J.	A	7
Anderson, II. II.	E	17	Blackman, George.	C	2
Abele, E.	C	10	Bryan, D. B.	C	7
Archibald, Thomas.	G	15	Blackwilder, J. A.	J	7
Anderson. Henry	D	18	Bryan, A.	A	7
Alston, Edward A.	F	15	Busby, J. W	G	7
Ames, John	K	18	Bass, R.	B	9
Arnold, G V.	D	19	Berry, Thomas S.	D	18
Athey, B. F.	D	15	Bowman, Lewis L.	I	10
Atkins, George E.	B	17	Berry, Columbus.	F	10
Anthony, W. B.	H	7	Betts, William.	D	10
Asherhurst, A. or M.	Johnson'sCav.		Barrett, D. A.	I	10
Brown, I. II.	Unknown.		Brewster, John C.	G	18
Barnham, S. P.	E	17	Black, John	C	10
Burk, B.	B	18	Barney, James.	H	11
Brown, A. J.		8	Brookman. James.	A	15
Barnett, D. A.	I	10	Bellamy, Marion	II	10
Barkam, J. C.	G	7	Bryant, Allen.	B	15

Name.	Co.	Reg't.
Bennet, William H	B	10
Busk, B	B	18
Binkner, John	F	18
Bures, E. S	K	17
Barber, Allen T	B	17
Baker, W. R	D	18
Bingham, A. G	B	17
Babbitt, James	F	10
Bothe, William	K	15
Bell, John Y	I	15
Bracker, J. A	G	10
Buckner, M. M	E	17
Braditt, W. K	C	10
Ball, L. G	K	15
Barrin, Isaac	D	18
Barrett, John J	A	17
Burden, Joseph	H	19
Bald, James E	A	17
Barefield, H	K	18
Butter, J. S	B	17
Bigmer, David	D	18
Bradley, Melvin	K	18
Berry, Samuel F	D	15
Broad, W. H	E	18
Blevin, G. W	D	18
Butler, J. R	A	10
Bulbard, L	G	10
Barnes, Huston	G	9
Carter, James	C	7
Camp, J. G	B	7
Cantrell, G. P	C	7
Clanbon, James	G	2
Cotterill, William	I	10
Cambell, S. R	C	17
Chrisman, William	I	15
Cruse, William A	C	18
Chambers, W. J	K	15
Colman, T. J	Det.	Co. Spies.
Craig, Frank	E	18
Cook, A. D. or M. D	B	15
Craft, James	F	18
Cruuk, Bird	B	17
Carothers, J. D	C	18
Crowman, W. S., or Crowson	K	17
Cash, George C	G	15
Chaffin, John T	G	17
Clark, A. M	F	10
Capel, Thomas	A	17
Cleveland, T. J	G	10
Cobb, James H	K	17
Coleman, William T	C	15
Christopher, B. T	C	15
Craig, G. L	K	17
Coleman, Theodore B	B	15
Clinton, J. R	G	17
Cooper, M. L	A	18
Cooper, E. F	A	18
Clifton, E. W	E	10
Corgill, John	B	10
Cox, James M	G	17
Campbell, John P	B	10
Cross, James W	D	18
Cox, William M	I	18
Carey, William C	F	10

Name.	Co.	Reg't.
Campbell, Squier	D	10
Cook, Andrew R	G	15
Carter, J. W	C	10
Casey, Richard F	H	10
Collins, J. S	K	18
Chambliss, P. A	K	18
Campbell, Thomas	E	23
Cogwell, William	F	10
Crum, William	I	18
Crosbey, G	I	25
Collins, William	K	30
Chambler, P. A	K	10
Cooper, W. H	D	15
Chappel, Thomas	G	10
Cinonell, Daniel	K	10
Craig, J. L	H	17
Donald, Irving	C	7
Duffey, D	I	18
Dubarry, Thomas J	C	17
Durnett, William	B	15
Dean, Charles D	D	17
Davis, James U	A	18
Dunham, William O	G	18
Davis, Nathan	E	17
Derden, Henry J	K	18
Doride, Monroe, or Doude	C	18
Dodson, J. R	E	17
Dickson, W. B	E	10
Dawson, J. T	B	15
Driscoll, S. J	I	5
Darnell, William I	B	15
Duffy, William	I	18
Donaldson, A. J	B	17
Everett, R. C	K	7
Evans, H. R	D	17
Ewing, John	C	18
Evans, John	I	15
Early, Thomas	D	18
Engeldon, Creed	A	17
Elliott, Thomas	D	18
Eddenson, R	E	10
Embrey, Enoch G	K	10
Embrey, W O	B	17
Early, John W	I	18
English, Wayne D	H	15
Enmon, Isaiah	C	10
Epperson, S	K	8
Edwardson or Edwinson, James	F	10
Elliot, C. B	C	15
Ernst, George I	C	10
Edmonson, James	F	10
English, Creed	A	17
Everett, R. C	H	7
Ellis, W. J	E	Unknown
Evans, M. R	D	17
Faqua, J. W	G	10
Ford, H. C	K	17
Fuston, M. W	E	17
Frankersley, J. R	D	15
Farrell, Thomas	C	10
Framel, John	I	15
Ferrill, T	B	17
Fisher, Wesley	F	10

Name.	Co.	Reg't.
Featherson, W. H.	K	18
Files, A. A	K	18
Fullerton, William A.	B	10
Falkner, Jim	K	18
Finley, James II	I	15
Ferrin, H. F	K	17
Freeman, Tyer	B	13
Futeril, D. J	C	18
Fuller, C. F. or C. L.	G	14
Fry, W. B	B	10
Gorney, A. M	E	7
Gibbs, John F	A	17
Graham, S W	I	18
Gibberth, James	B	17
Gray, J. S	G	10
Glen, William	D	10
Gravett, J. M	K	18
Granberry, R.P. or R.C.	H	17
Goodman, John F	D	10
Garrett, B	B	18
Gilbreth, James	C	17
Green, J. W	K	17
Goodgion, L. S	A	18
Grimes, David	B	17
Green, William H	Johnson's Co. Spies, Cav.	
Griffin, John F	D	13
Garrother, John D	C	18
Grimes, Daniel	B	17
Glasgow, W. P	I	50
Gilbrath, James	B	17
Goodwin, John F	D	10
Harrison, A. J	E	7
Havery, Brown	I	7
Hammett, George	B	3
Heim, Laf., darkey	H	7
Huggins, G. W	E	7
Hicks, H. D.	A	7
Higinbotham, J. N	I	7
Hamilton, J	E	12
Hawthorn, A	I	18
Hawkins, G. W	E	10
Hayten, J. J	H	17
Henderson, L. A	B	Richards' Cavalry.
Hawley, M. C., L. C. right initials		Richards' Cavalry.
Hayes, J. M	D	15
Hearl, Thomas B	A	18
Hamilton, Berry	H	17
Hambright, R. L	A	10
Hudson, Ira	B	15
Hogland, Henry	G	10
Hawes, Thomas	C	18
Hines, J. D	G	17
Hyde, John	B	18
Holloway, Sidney	H	15
Harris, William	K	17
Haggard, James	E	10
Hopper, L. C	E	15
Hambreek, George B.	I	15
Haley, James C	B	15
Hanna, John M	E	10
Harrison, J. R	A	18

Name.	Co.	Reg't.
Howard, W. T	B	17
Havis, D. G	K	17
Hendricks, Willis R.	B	8
Miller, T. B	H	17
Holmes, G. W	D	17
Howell, John	B	15
Hessin, Berry O	H	15
Hawsley, J. J	I	17
Harris, H	D	10
Holloway, William H.	F	15
Hale, David E	H	10
Hart, A. W	H	8 Cav.
Horton, James S	D	17
Hopkins, I	A	14
Hardaway, Oliver	H	3
Hynson, J. C	E	17
Hilton, John	G	7
Harris, S. G	K	17
Harris, W. J	B	10
Herne, L	H	7
Hanley, N. J	D	2
Hinkland, W. H.	D	17
Hicks, M	Johnson's Sqd.	
Hey, W. J	H	18
Irby, Stephen D	C	18
Inman, C	A	15
Jones, James W	C	10
Johnston, Emery	F	17
Johnston, William L.	E	18
Jordan, John.	C	18
Jackson, James	F	10
Jacques, S. F. Rev	F	10
Jones, John	F	18
Jumany, Carroll	A	15
Jarrott, J. M	K	17
Jordan, William F	B	10
Jordan David	C	18
Joy, William B	E	10
Jones, Hiram J. R	B	10
Johnson, P. N	C	15
James, Hamilton	E	12
Kennard, D. S	C	10
Kirkland, W. H	D	17
Kelly, James	D	16
King, Thomas H	H	17
Key, C	K	17
Kinlon, J. T	E	15
Kinney, William T	D	14
Karney, T. W	K	32
Kothies, J. E	K	18
Kimes, W. E.	D	18
King, James B	G	15
Kingammon, D. M	C	50
Kinston, J. T	E	15
Koger, L. H	Johnson'sCav.	
Lewis, V. L	G	7
Lee, J. B	G	7
Lively, P	E	18
Lockridge, W. J	G	10
Leastrunk, T. W	E	17
Lewis, William	K	15
Lowery, A. P	C	17
Lawson, S. F	H	17
Lee, Jackson M	C	17
Lowe, W. A	H	10

Name.	Co.	Reg't.
Long, William	B	17
Leavitt, John	F	10
Ledbetter, A. B.	I	10
Linsley, Henry	A	15
Louck, Thomas C.	C	18
Little, Thomas B.	G	17
Longley, M. L.	G	10
Logan, Robert S.	H	10
Lippert, G. W.	H	7
Mitchell, G. W.	Johnson'sCav.	
McGarcey, James.	K	10
Meadows, H. D.	H	7
Mellkany, R. H.	H	10
McFagg, John	G	10
McLain, C.	K	17
Moon, J.	F	15
McAncon, John	A	18
McCreight, T. N.	K	15
Mathews, W. B.	B	18
Mix, William H.	E	18
McJephen, Robert H.	H	10
McLain, C. W.	H	18
Miller, J. F.	D	1 Bat. Wall Legion.
McNabb, David R.	A	1
Moore, Jesse R	H	18
Miller, C.	B	9
McLean, James H	K	15
Mattoon, Granville H	E	18
Martin, I. T.	A	1
McAdams, H. D.	H	7
Manning, Joseph	G	7
McPhail, William	D	7
Mills, James A.	I	7
McMillan, J. Z.	H	7
Modrall, W. B.	H	7
Martin, W. R.	E	7
McIndale, James	C	7
Moore, J. C.	C	7
Mason, Robert	F	10
Manley, H. B.	I	10
McGarey, James	H	10
McCurty, John	E	10
Mattocks, George	B	15
Middleton, Nathan	D	15
McFall, L. M.	B	10
McAnnear, John	A	18
McLarein, J. M.	B	18
Montgomery, J. A.	A	10
Mason, Abner A.	B	18
Manning, W. B.	C	18
McKnight, Andrew	E	10
McMinn, V.	A	15
Morgan, George W.	I	18
Mugg, W. H. H.	E	15
Mathews, James C.	I	17
McDancel, W. H.	I	18
McKee, W. H.	I	1 Legion
McLean, James H.	K	15
McMellin, William	H	17
Marr, Henry W.	H	10
Mitchen, E. M.	K	18
Martin, John D	D	17
McClure, James M.	C	17
McGinire, M. W.	E	15

Name.	Co.	Reg't.
McAley, Aaron.	C	15
Malone, G. H.	E	18
Manier, R. W.	I	17
Matthews, W. R.	B	10
Miller, Thomas F.	G	15
Mills, Perry.	B	15
Martin, D. S.	G	15
McKinney, James P.	G	17
Murphy William.	C	10
McLane, Cornelius W.	K	18
McBright, Thomas.	K	15
Mathis, Robert.	E	15
Morrison, J. T.	C	10
Miller, G. W.	E	18
Nichols, L. M.	I	7
Nelson, M. N.	B	17
Newton, Fleming.	G	17
Neil, William G.	E	17
Nick, David	F	18
Nelson, Daniel H.	C	18
Neals, William.	E	18
Nelson, W. V.	B	17
Owen, John.	K	18
O'Barr, R. T.	A	15
Oakely, William D.	Johnson'sCav.	
Obans, Peter	A	15
Oden, George.	E	17
Potter, J. R.	F	7
Priest, W. K.	E	3
Potts, D. M.	B	7
Priest, K. M.	E	7
Potter, J. C.	F	7
Patton, William.	C	10
Price, George.	C	17
Pickens, M. J.	C	18
Paten, John (colored).	I	17
Price, B. F.	C	17
Pienfro, John W.	C	10
Peters, David.	F	18
Putreel, D. A.	C	18
Patton, James.	C	17
Pendegrast, Newton.	C	17
Perkins, H. E.	E	15
Phelps, E.	D	17
Persons, A. T.	F	15
Perry, Thomas.	E	17
Patrick, E.	E	15
Preston, George W.	Johnson'sCav.	
Parham, S. P.	E	17
Payton, G. L., or Paton	B	18
Price, Merida.	D	15
Pierson, W. C.	C	14
Phillips, William T.	B	15
Phenix, James R.	B	17
Pinkerton, J. M.	B	17
Pearl, Willis.	H	10
Pennington, John.	D	18
Poiner, S. M.	H	17
Pichards, John.	F	18
Prithard, W. L.	H	11
Pearce, Thomas B.		15 Legion
Print, I.	F	2
Parker, Ransom	F	15
Pollock, C.	D	18
Peoples, J. R.	F	15

Name.	Co.	Reg't.
Pevey, G. W	H	15
Payten	K	17
Powell, J. C	E	10
Peale, Robert B	C	15
Riggin, G. F	D	4
Riddle, J. M	I	7
Reed, C. F	F	7
Rea, James	C	7
Richey, G. W	I	7
Robinson, Asa	H	10
Ring, J. B	G	15
Reynolds, E. T	B	17
Robertson, John	C	17
Rigger, T. J	A	18
Reynolds, James A	F	15
Roberts, D. T. S	D	10
Rogers, J. W	G	16
Robinson, William	K	10
Rogers, E. W	B	15
Rogers, R. C. C	A	18
Robertson, Peter	F	18
Reynolds, William M	A	18
Roeark, William F	E	18
Rominy, Thomas N., or Romaine	B	18
Rose, Zack M	D	17
Ring, W. J	B	10
Ramsay, C. S	C	18
Ross, Thomas B	H	10
Ridge, James H	B	10
Rimes, W. E	D	18
Robinson, Benjamin	I	10
Richards, John	F	18
Robinson, L. M	D	14
Rattitt, George	F	10
Ray, James	C	17
Ruffin, Thomas	I	19
Renford, W. J	E	48
Rickards, J	E	18
Robinson, P	F	15
Roberts, W	I	10
Rogers, L. H		Johnson'sCav.
Snipes, J. G	C	7
Scott, T. J	B	7
Smith, R. E	F	7
Strong, S. W	I	7
Streeter, S. J	G	7
Skiles, B	H	7
Stewart, H. B	G	7
Surraville. J. B	G	7
Smith, William	I	3
Sharp, W. S	H	7
Smith, B. F	H	7
Sidwell, Baker	C	18
Scott, A. W	K	18
Sinclair, Thomas	A	18
Sharp, W. N	F	15
Sprinkle, J. S	E	15
Starkyan, J. W	C	18
Smith, James R	E	10
Stockard, F. N	E	17
Sparks, William	E	18
Smith, James	G.	18
Sewell, James S	I	15
Summers, Thomas	B	18

Name.	Co.	Reg't.
Smith, William H.	C	18
Stock, Jas. S. or J. G.	B	6
Self, Asa	B	17
Staley, Samson	K	18
Seals, Thomas	F	10
Sweeney, James	B	Taylor's Reg't.
Sammanel, J. W	K	18
Stiles, J. M	F	18
Shannon, William S	C	10
Sparkes, H. S	G	18
Scott, Walter M	E	18
Strait, J H	E	19
Still, Jacob	H	15
Smith, Edwin	A	10
Smith, Edward	I	17
Shuslock, Malion	A	18
Sigler, G. W	G	18
Slover, J. J	B	17
Stewart, William	K	15
Stillen, George C	C	17
Smith, James	A	10
Sellers, B. F	F	18
Slimer, J. N	K	10
Smith, John G	B	7
Smith, C. H	C	3
Spurlock, M. V	A	18
St. John, W. W	C	41
Studdard, I. N	E	17
Sheen, William	D	10
Sidbottam, M	I	15
Smith, J. R	E	10
Singston, J M	B	17
Stockton, J. P	C	18
Streer, S J	C	17
Shiles, V	H	7
Snipps, J. G	C	7
Seeley, P. L	G	18
Seasetrunk, J. W	C	17
Sypert, J. W	H	7
Thompson, William C.	B	7
Thorne, James	F	7
Tailor, Thomas D	B	15
Truelove, Tim	C	17
Treadwell, W. H., or Tidwell	B	10
Taylor, R. A	K	10
Turney, D. D	E	15
Taylor, W. O	K	17
Towells, J. C	E	10
Tramel, Daniel J	E	15
Taylor, A. H	F	18
Taylor, Thomas	E	15
Tidwell, Lewis G	A	10
Thorn, C. A	A	17
Tidwell, Franklin	F	10
Tankersly, D. B	D	15
Tankerly, J. W	C	15
Tredwell, Benjamin F.	H	17
Tisdale, R. M	E	32
Toney, John	K	17
Tidwell, T. J	F	10
Terry, Thomas	E	17
Turraville, J. B	G	7
Taylor, R. Y.	K	10

Name.	Co.	Reg't.
Talley, S. G.	D	7
Tankersly, J. R.	D	15
Underwood, J. G.	I	17
Underwood, J. W.	I	17
Underwood, J. S.	I	17
Unknown Prisoner	B	19
Wilkinson, J. M.	B	7
Wetherby, E. R.	D	7
Wetherby, J. T.	F	7
Ward, S. M.	E	7
Winn, J P.	H	7
Walker, Sam S.	D	15
White, Thomas I.	I	15
Ward, George	A	15
Walker, A. T. or A. J.	K	17
Williams, W. A.	B	17
Woods, James S.	G	10
Wetherby, John	H	17
Watkins, J. A.	I	15
Walker, Martin V.	K	15
Wilton, W. H.	B	15
Ware, James B.	E	18

Name.	Co.	Reg't.
Work, Robert F.	D	15
Winn, P. T.	K	18
Williams, W. H.	C	15
Watkins, T. G.	G	17
Walker, John F.	B	10
Wilson, Frank M.	C	17
Wakefield, Thomas A.	G	18
Wait, Thomas	K	15
Ward, W. A. R. D.	I	10
Wilson, J. M.	K	15
Ward, Samuel T.	K	15
White, D. C.	F	15
Wyman, J. C.	E	17
Wallace, Thomas J. or William J.	I	17
Walker, Thomas J.	I	17
Walker, Benjamin	H	32
Walker, R. M.	K	18
Weats, William	E	18
Weatherly, J. F.	E	7
Witts, W.	H	14
Young, Solomon	K	15

VIRGINIA.

Aggregate dead 187, classified as follows:

INFANTRY.

From 1st Regiment		2
" 2d "		4
" 4th "		1
" 5th "		2
" 9th "		2
" 10th "		1
" 21st "		2
" 25th "		2
" 27th "		2
" 36th "		1
" 37th "		2
" 46th "		1
" 54th "		8
" 55th "		1
" 56th "		1
" 60th "		1

INFANTRY.

From 63d Regiment		6
" 64th "		132
" 65th "		1
" 66th "		1
Conscripts		2
Citizen		1

CAVALRY.

From 1st Regiment		4
" 7th "		2

ARTILLERY.

From French's Battery		3
" Virginia "		1
" Floyd's "		1

DETAILS.

Name.	Co.	Reg't.	Name.	Co	Reg't.
Arnold, J. E.	G	64	Carter, D. W.	C	64
Bamfrance, W. J.	I	64	Coleman, William L.		63
Buckner, M.	D	64	Carrol, W. J.	A	64
Berry, J. V.	C	61	Chillen, Elijah	C	64
Barnett, J. T. or H. T.	C	2	Clark, Isaac	E	63
Barnes, S.	K	64	Corwall, J. B.	B	61
Bryant, J. R.	D	64	Dickinson, J. W.	K	64
Broadwater, J.	E	64	Doss, William	A	1
Berry, John A.	C	64	Davis, John	I	64
Boatwright, W. B.	C	1 Cav.	Davis, James	G	64
Bedney, D. B.	A	64	Duff, William	B	64
Baler, George	C	27	Elkins, W. W. B.	H	64
Black, James R.	A	54	Eladge, William	B	55
Brickey, D. M.	E	64	Elkins, Joseph M.	K	61
Brown, N. J.	A	64	Erzel, Samuel	B	64
Comer, John		French's Art.	Fisher, John		French's Art.
Carter, M. C.	C	64	Furron,J.F..or Furrow	I	54
Carson, J.	D	56	Farley, J. H.	B	64
Clarke, W.	F or H	64	Frame, Llewellyn		Conscript.
Cannon, J. C.	B	64	Fry, Robert		1 Cav.
Custer, Isaac	B	7 Cav.	Fry, John	E	1
Clifton, William	K or I	64	Frazer, William	C	64
Creach, A. L.	A	64	Fletcher, I	D	64
Collins, Noah	E	64	Field, F.	B	64
Crumley, Samuel		64	Ganott, M.	A	64
Church, Isaiah	K	64	Grubb, B. E., or Grabb	B	64
Calahan, Edward	F	64	Garrott, M.	A	64
Carter, Ransom	I	64	Gibson, William	E	64

Name.	Co.	Reg't.	Name.	Co	Reg't.
Gray, M	C	1	Parsons, Geo. or John.		Floyd's Art'
Goldsmith, William	A	64	Parsons, George	A	21
Galsenberg, Chas	G	64	Phipps, J., or Philips.	B	2
Harris, Marmaduke	C	64	Philips, John P	B	7 Cav.
Hensley, W. H	D	64	Pennett, C. W	E	37
Henshaw, L. M	B	64	Parsons, W	G	64
Holstar, Floyd	C	2	Poteels, D	B	61
Hobbs, Aaron S	G	64	Penning, A. I	A	64
Hall, A. C	B	64	Paunell, Joseph	E	64
Hyatt, Eli W	I	64	Pravers, William	B	64
Hayes, John	A	4 Batt'n.	Phrame, L		Conscript.
Hall, J. P., or Hail	I	64	Parsons, Z	A	21
Harliss, J	I	64	Quesenberg, C	G	64
Hilton, A	A	64	Russell, E. P or T. R.	G	64
Harris, M	D	64	Rosenbaum, W. H		Citizen.
Hill, John	D	64	Rivers, William	A	64
Higgins, David	C	63	Russell, L. D	G	64
Helley, James	B	64	Rinser, George	F	61
Head, J. H	D	64	Rucker, Daniel	A	64
Harrison, Henry	B	64	Rutlidge, G. G	H	64
Harris, James	G	64	Rhodes, James	C	65
Ingle, I. or A	K	64	Ramsay, J. A	A	64
Ingle, John	F	61	Shoup, G. W	G	64
Johnson, Gordon	G	64	Standa, D. T	B	64
James, Henry	H	64	Seamon, D. S	E	25
Jayne, John	A	64	Sally, M., or saeley	I	64
Jones, A. T	H	64	Smith, Ed	G	64
Justis, James	E	54	Shelton, J. S	D	60
Johnson, B	G	64	Sloan, G. W	C	61
Jones, H	H	64	Stridham, A	A	64
Kruggs, J. S., or Kaggs.	A	64	Sartin, A. J	D	36
Kimberly, J. S	D	64	Sloan, James	C	64
Kline, T. C	B	64	Snodgrass, William M.	B	63
King, James A	E	54	Suplene, John	E	64
Kinzer, George	F	64	Stephens, Henry C	ii	64
Lane, James E	D	64	Smith, W	A	64
Lark, Joseph	B	64	Spaulding, Bryant	D	66
Lloyd, W. C	K	63	Springle, William	B	64
Leamon, B L	E	25	Smith, Aleck	A	64
Moore, William	H	64	Sloan, H	G	64
Moore, B	F	64	Spangler, Abraham	D	64
McLaughlin, J		1 Cav.	Sumner, William	B	10
McClure, Enoch	C	64	Sewer, B	B	5
Muness, Huston	C	64	Thornton, Thomas B.		French's Ar
McKinney, David	A	64	Travis, J	G	64
McCoy, Pleasant	A	5	Tipton, C. or J	C	64
Martin, J. F	E	64	Thacker, M	D	64
Murphy, R. S	C	61	Terry, Joseph		27
McConnell, S. C	E	61	Thomas, J. W	I	61
Maxwell, A	B	64	Thomas, Charles	H	64
Maxwell, H. B	B	64	Tompkins, B. T	H	64
Mondy, P		Virginia Bat.	Venable, A	C	64
Minton, Joseph	I	37	Whetlock, A	A	54
Murphy, Anderson	C	64	Williams, E. H	F	2
Miller, James	A	64	Watts, Granville	C	54
Martin, S. F	E	16	Waddell, J	A	9
Noe, James	B	64	Wilson, Marion	H	64
Nolls, John	B	64	Wells, James	G	64
Napier, P	K	64	Watkins, George	C	64
Noe, Solomon	B	64	Wood Richard	G	64
Noddle, Jefferson	A	9	Waddle, J. F	B	54
Noe, Joseph	B	64	Wildreth, Andrew J	H	63
Olinger, Calvin	K	64	Woodward, John	K	64
Orr, Henry W	F	64	Welsh, James	G	61
Owen, H	C	64	Young, David	K	64

FLORIDA.

Aggregate dead **24**, classified as follows :

INFANTRY.

From 1st Regiment		5
" 3d "		2
" 4th "		7
" 6th "		6

INFANTRY.

From 14th Regiment		2
" 33d "		1
" 64th "		1

DETAILS.

Name.	Co.	Reg't.	Name.	Co.	Reg't.
Brehel, Richard	E	1	Lanmore, W	E	4
Blakeman, A	I	6	Lawster, J	E	6
Barefoot, Thomas	B	1	Latner, L. R	C	4
Bentroe, Casper	C	14	Larrimore, William	E	4
Cobin, John	I	1	Moat, J. W	C	1
Callahan, Thomas	H	33	Mercer, J. H	F	6
Conrad, D. S	D	6	Pappy, John	B	3
Dowdy, Benjamin	F	1	Renfue, James	F	14
Hall, S. J	C	3	Winget, R. B	F	4
Jewell, Dan W	D	6	Walker, John D	D	1
Knight, W. L	F	4	Wells, J	G	4
Latner, L. K		64	Ward, E. J	I	6

LOUISIANA.

Aggregate dead **78**, classified as follows:

<table>
<tr><td colspan="3">INFANTRY.</td><td colspan="3">INFANTRY.</td></tr>
<tr><td>From 1st Regiment</td><td></td><td>6</td><td>From 58th Regiment</td><td></td><td></td></tr>
<tr><td>" 4th</td><td>"</td><td>5</td><td>" Naval Brigade</td><td></td><td></td></tr>
<tr><td>" 12th</td><td>"</td><td>2</td><td colspan="3"></td></tr>
<tr><td>" 13th</td><td>"</td><td>13</td><td colspan="3">CAVALRY.</td></tr>
<tr><td>" 16th</td><td>"</td><td>6</td><td colspan="3"></td></tr>
<tr><td>" 17th</td><td>"</td><td>1</td><td>From 1st Regiment</td><td></td><td></td></tr>
<tr><td>" 18th</td><td>"</td><td>3</td><td>" 3d</td><td>"</td><td></td></tr>
<tr><td>" 19th</td><td>"</td><td>3</td><td colspan="3"></td></tr>
<tr><td>" 20th</td><td>"</td><td>5</td><td colspan="3">ARTILLERY.</td></tr>
<tr><td>" 25th</td><td>"</td><td>2</td><td>From Pt. Coupee Battery</td><td></td><td></td></tr>
<tr><td>" 30th</td><td>"</td><td>2</td><td>" Hoover's 1st Regiment</td><td></td><td></td></tr>
<tr><td>" 36th</td><td>"</td><td>1</td><td>" Washington Artillery</td><td></td><td></td></tr>
<tr><td>" 53d</td><td>"</td><td>1</td><td>" 4th Battery</td><td></td><td></td></tr>
<tr><td>" 55th</td><td>"</td><td>2</td><td>" Unknown Batteries</td><td></td><td></td></tr>
</table>

DETAILS.

Name.	Co.	Reg't.
Anaker, S	Pt.	Coupee Art.
Braner, H., or Bremer.	B	13
Budrow, James		Hoover's 1st Artillery.
Barton. John	I	1
Becker, George	C	30
Brideshaw, Henry	F	53
Bedford, Thomas E.	E	1 Cav.
Bradford, J R	H	Washington Art.
Callum, Burnett	B	1 Art.
Calcoat, J. H	D	25
Coe, James S	G	16
Calwah, John H	C	25
Carter, C. H	I	4
Cooper, William C.	B	16
Cox, Abraham	A	16
Cavillon, P. H	G	1
Dunn, W. F	I	16
Daley, Pat	G	1 Cav.
Davis, John	F	1
Dillon, P	A	1
Derrena, Mitchell	K	18
Edwards, T. S	C	16
Fonder, G	C	20
Fisher, William C		Naval Brigade
Froide, Green	I	1
Gilliland, William	D	12
Goodard, W. G	H	36

Name.	Co.	Reg't.
Goodrich, J. F	E	Bat.
Gibson, A. J		3 Cav.
Harris, J. H		Pt. Coupee A
Herman, Albert	B	20
Hoolgood, H	G	4
Justiss. B. H	C	19
Johnson, S. M	D	20
Kennedy, Pat	H	18
Kinchin, J. J., or Kitchen		Pt. Coupee A
Kennedy, L	D	13
Kennedy, J. B	K	55
Kenney, P	A	20
Levi, M		Pt. Conpee A
Lunchford, J. S	D	17
Lisk, G		Washington Artillery.
Long, A	B	1
Lisson, John	B	3 Cav.
Lyons, John	D	13
McCarroll, Webster	G	13
Meredith, Robert		Pt. Coupee A
McDonald, T. W	H	13
McAdams, R. F	E	19
Maldott, G. L	D	58
Nicholson, Thomas	I	13
Neil, E. D	G	4
Price, G	I	13
Palmer, J. R	I	1 Cav.

Name.	Co.	Reg't.
Fortman, John	H	20
Phelps, William C.	C	4
Pulcher, Adam	B	... Bat.
Price, H.	I	13
Roach, Anthony	C	4 Bat.
Robinson, William	G	1
Robertson, Joseph	I	12
Stephens, C. J.	...	... Art.
Stringer, S.	F	18
Smith, E. L.	H	16
Seglers, J.	E	13
Smith, William	E	19
Shippey, John	H	13

Name.	Co.	Reg't.
Turley, W. F., or Tuley	D	16
Triod, Orane	I	1 Art.
Voyles, J. R.	D	55
White, Abraham	D	13
West, George	I	13
Womauer, Joseph, or Wommer	I	13
Ward, Joseph E.	F	30
Webb, C. W.	B	... Bat.
Watson, J. F.	...	.. Bat.
Wolt, James H.	B	3 Cav.
Warren, Foster	H	1 Cav.

MISSOURI.

Aggregate dead **26**, classified as follows:

INFANTRY.				CAVALRY.		
From 1st Regiment		4		From 3d Regiment		.
" 2d "		1		" 6th "		...
" 3d "		2		" 8th "		
" 4th "		1				
" 5th "		3		ARTILLERY.		
" 6th "		3				
" 9th "		1		From 1st Battery		..
" 10th "		1		" 2d "		
Unknown		1				
Conscript		1				
Citizen		1				

DETAILS.

Name.	Co.	Reg't.	Name.	Co.	Reg't.
Allen, R. N. or P. N.		1 Art.	Knight, J.	D	6
Boze, A. C.		Citizen.	Leggins, George	F	5
Cecil, A. H. B.	J	1	McRae, Alexander	B	3 Cav.
Dunkle, R. A.	H	1	Myers, J. H.	I	1
Dorris, T. F.	K	..	Nichols, D. C.	A	3 Cav.
Ellis, T. H.	E	3 Cav.	Proser, D.	H	5
Eads, Riley	E	4	Philips, Joseph	A	9
Grant, William A.	I	1	Parker, J. V.	B	5
Hoppert, J. H.	H	6 Cav.	Rowden, J. H. ....H or	I	8 Cav.
Hulley, F. M.		2 Bat.	Sidebottom, M.	D	2
Houston, B. F.	H	6	Spurlock, Nathan	H	10
Hopper, J H.	E	6	Taber, J. C.	H	3
Jackson, J. C.	I	Conscript.	White, J. S.	C	3

l

SOUTH CAROLINA.

Aggregate dead 13, classified as follows:

INFANTRY.		INFANTRY.	
From 1st Regiment	2	From 16th Regiment	1
" 3d "	1	" 24th "	7
" 10th "	1	" 62d "	1

DETAILS.

Name.	Co.	Reg't.	Name.	Co.	Reg't.
Barnes, N	H	24	McKee, R	E	1
Breeling, J	D	24	McGee, S W	B	24
Chunby, G. W., or			Smith, H J		16
Chumley	K	3	Timmerman, T. A	K	24
George, J. L	K	24	Turner, Thomas	F	10
Hager, Daniel	B	1	Wallace, M	H	24
Hill, John A	F	62	Walker, J. D	E	24

MISCELLANEOUS COMMANDS.

Aggregate dead **218**, classified as follows:

DETAILS.

ARIZONA

Name.	Co.	Reg't.
Miles, James	G	1
Wells, Joseph S	G	1

FIRST TENNESSEE, MISSISSIPPI AND ALABAMA.

Name.	Co.	Reg't.
Burratt, Jacob	G	
Beard, T.W.	I	
Brane, J. M	H	
Bloodworth, J.	F	
Bard, J. W	I	
Gibson, L J. A		
Hubbard, R.	I	
Hammer, T V	H	
Kennedy,J		
Randall, James	D	
Randall, F. M	H	

Name.	Co.	Reg't.
Ray, T. M	B	
Scott, Jesse	K	
Scott, F. J	D	
Whittle, W. H	B	
Wade, J. F		

FORREST'S CAVALRY.

Name.	Co.	Reg't.
Braker, Joseph		
Brazier, J		
Goolsby, E		
Green, James I		
Gray, A R		Scout.
Hyatt,William		
Snow, Samuel		
Thornton, J		Escort.
Wade, J. F		Escort.
Williams, A. D		Scout.

SUNDRY COMMANDS.

Adcock, N. E., Combs' Battalion.
Ater, Jasper, a citizen.
Alexander, J. F., Ross' Artillery.
Ankemizen, an Indian.
Allan, J. A , Newman's Bat.
Atkinson, W., Co. and Reg't unk'n.
Ardwin, J., Co. and Reg't unknown.
Brewer, W M., D, Heavy Artillery.
Bryant, J. H., Cumberland Artillery.
Bogues, J., A, 7 Confederates.
Blackwell, A T., E, 3 Confederates.
Bennefield, H., F, 8 Confederates.
Burke, Frank, Muckerson's Bat.
Boatwright, W. B., C, 1 Cavalry.
Baker, William, Powell's Regiment.
Bamtall, J. G., Baxter's Bat.
Bour. J. L., Foiler's Bat.

Barton, John W., Haskin's Company.
Boek, Thos., Co. and Reg't unknown.
Beck.Presley,Co and Reg't unknown.
Boggs, Joseph. A, Pettoes' Company.
Boyd, Jos., Co. and Reg't unknown.
Boone, A. J., Co. 1 Confederates.
Cusick, Michael, B, Floating Battery.
Cook, E., or Cox, Belmont Battery.
Cannon, J. C., Williams' Battery.
Carrol, David, D 3 Confed. Cavalry.
Childers, George. K, Walker's Battalion, Jackson's Brigade.
Coffee,Wm. M.,Co. & Reg't unknown.
Chandler, J. C., Canton's Company.
Castleman, Ira, Baxter's Battalion.
Colley, Madison, Terrant's Bat.
Childers, John, K, Walker's Bat.

Choates, S., Co. and Reg't unknown.
Craig, J. L., Co. and Reg't unknown.
Daniels, W W., 1, Rhodes' Reg.
Davis, A J., Dorson Bat.
Dockray, J. N., Co. & Reg't unknown.
Ellis, W. J., Co. and Reg't unknown.
Elkins, Harvey, K, Prentice's Batt'n.
Epperson, Wm., Co. & Reg't unknown.
Elms, J. H., Robertson's Bat.
Eddy, A., A, Reg't unknown.
Fitzgeralo, R. F., a citizen.
Freer, Lewis, Cumberland Artillery.
Ferril, R. H., Baxter's Battery.
Ferguson, Eli H , H, Herald's Bat.
Foamell, A. O., G. Hill's Dragoons.
Foss, J. B., Co. and Reg't unknown.
Frick, S. M., Co. and Reg't unknown.
Gilchrist, A. R., E, 10 Confederate.
Gibbon, Thos. J., Co.& Reg't unknown.
Galaway, T., 1. 16 Confederate.
Gray, Thomas B., Powell's Bat.
Gastin, James, K. 55 Confederate.
Grouter, W. J., K, 1 Confederate.
Griffey, Owen, Co. & Reg't unknown.
Grant, Joseph, Co. & Reg't unknown.
Goodwin, B. J., Murray's Artillery.
Horton, J. F., Roker's Battery.
Harberson, J. M., Ross' Artillery.
Holt, Jefferson, Cumberland Art'y.
Holloway, J., Ghants' Cavalry.
Hudson, Thos. Y., Richardson's Cav.
Hale, F. H., Fraiman's Battery.
Henry, William, Colson's Command.
Hartell, James M , — 14 Confederate.
Hendricks, J , Franklin Battalion.
Hett, S. M., K, 16 Confederate.
Hendricks, David L.,Co & Reg't unk'n
Henry, T. B, Smith's Bat.
Hargrove, Allen, Sullivan's Battery.
Hutchins, Lewis W., C, 1 Confederate.
Henrot, A. J., Thompson's Bat.
Haynes, D., Haine's Regiment.
Holloway, S. M., K, 3 Confederate.
Hurst, William, Freeman's Bat.
Hooley, James, Co. and Reg't unk'n.
Henson, H. J., Co. and Reg't unk'n.
Hubbard, Allan, 1, Baker's Regiment.
Jordan, Martin, Co. and Reg't unk'n.
Johnson, M. S., Co. and Reg't unk'n.
Keaton, John, Ghants' Cavalry.
Keith, Robert, Dismuke's Artillery.
King, W. G., B or D 10 Confederate.
King, H. B., B, 10 Confederate.
Keating, Charles H., D. 16 Confed.
Keller, William, Co. and Reg't unk'n.
Kennard, M., Co. and Reg't unk'n.
Kutemeyer, John, Co. & Reg't unk'n.
Keims, D., Co. and Reg't unknown.
Lawton, W. J., B, 3 Confederate.
Lokey, W. B., C, 9 Confederate.
Lusk, J. W., A, 3 Confederate.
Lucas, Thomas, Co. and Reg't unk'n.
Lees, James H., Co. and Reg't unk'n.
Lord, Asa, B, 14 Confederate.
Linderman, J. R., Dole's Bat.
Lingrun, C. A., Co. and Reg't unk'n.

Lowell, J. L., Co. and Reg't unk'n.
Mansfield, Richard, Belmont Batt'y.
Maza, William, A, 1 Cavalry.
Martin, John, Co and Reg't unk'n.
McCloud, J. J., H. 10 Confederate.
McCracken, J., Philips' Legion.
Murr, A., Morton's Battery.
Murdoch, Chas. P., Crockett's Batt'n.
Moseley, M. H., Co. and Reg't unk'n.
Mooney, Frank, Hart's Battery.
Maunes, Hue, a citizen of Iowa.
McKary, James, U. S. Navy.
Mar, Robert B., B, 1 Confederate.
Mallicott, John, K. 10 Confederate.
Martin, John. B, Maxwell's Bat.
Milton, Mathew, E, 1 Confederate.
Malory, M., Co. and Reg't unknown.
McKibben, G., G, Munson's.
Manneyell, Holmes' Bat.
Mansfield, H., Belmont Bat.
Moore, J. F , Co. and Reg't unk'n.
Meck, H. M., Crew's Bat.
Milton, John, B, Murkeson's Bat.
Marues, S., Co. and Reg't unknown.
Nicholes, W. J., Co. and Reg't unk'n.
Nobler, M., G, 14 Cavalry.
Oxford, J J., Co. A,Confed. Reserves.
Pain, David A., Madrid Heavy Art'y.
Peyton, J., A, 1 Confederate.
Patterson, N. W., C, 3 Confederate.
Patton, W. M., Freeman's Regiment.
Procton, J. M , Stoneworth's Batt'y.
Poe, James, K, 3 Confederate.
Pace, John, Co and Reg't unknown.
Porter, John, Co. and Reg't unk'n.
Pardue, J. F., Darton's Bat.
Puifro, J. W., Co. and Reg't unk'n.
Pront, S., Co. and Reg't unknown.
Pence, E., Co. and Reg't unknown.
Roke, J. T., Rucker's Artillery.
Ryan, John, Gunboat Beauregard.
Rumsey, J. M., C, 1 Confederate.
Rogers, W. J , Owens' Bat.
Rogers, William, Roan's Bat.
Rose, N. P., Maloy Co.
Roberts, L , Co. and Reg't unknown.
Reynolds, James,Co.and Reg't unk'n.
Richey, P., A 23 Illinois.
Roeack, W., Co. and Reg't unknown.
Smith, Joseph, Crawford's Battalion.
Spink, R., Dismuke's Artillery.
Scott, Wm. C , Co. A,Jack May's Bat'n.
Shinluff, C. M., Co. and Reg't unk'n.
Siles, J. D., Darden's Battery.
Senton, Calvin, Herald's Bat.
See, J. H., H, 1 Confederate.
Saunders, A. M., Co. and Reg't unk'n.
Shellrot, Wm. A., A, Murkeson's Bat.
Stell, John, E, Elphuneworth's Bat.
Simms, R. J. M., Hardy's Bat.
Sherman, Luther, A, Powell's Bat.
Stephens, E., Co. and Reg't unk'n.
Sherry, Joseph, Co. and Reg't unk'n.
Schilknecht, J., Co. and Reg't unk'n.
Smith, H., Co. and Reg't unknown.
Smith, John, A. Richardson's Batt'y.

Smith, Joseph, Cross' Battalion.
Smith, William, Co. and Reg't unk'n.
Sewerly, John, Co. and Reg't unk'n.
Tompkins, John F., Murkeson's Bat.
Thompson, A., Murray's Bat.
Taylor, James, II, 1 Confederate.
Vandivere, James J., G, 28 Cavalry.
Wood, II., Crusen's Battalion.
Woodward, A. II., Baker's Regiment.
Winsman, A. J., G, 3 Confederate.
Welch, James, II, 1 Confederate.
Willey, Houston, Co. and Reg't unk'n.
Wells, John, Perrin's Regiment.

Wood, II., G, 1 Confederate.
Welcher, J. J., Co. and Reg't unk'n.
Weatherford, J. B., B Sand's Bat.
Walker, William, F, McGee Reg.
Walker, James T., Terrent's Battery.
Walker, R. A., G, 1 Confederate.
Wright, J. M., Murkeson's Bat.
Williams, Henry, Colston's Co.
Winget, R. B., F, 4 Artillery.
Winson, A. J., Co. and Reg't unk'n.
Walsh, G., Hadley's Bat.
Zoney, N. Z., Co. and Reg't unk'n.

[There are 36 names with company references on the records as members of the First Regiment Tennessee, Mississippi and Alabama, which are duplicates of names and companies from the several States, and consequently are omitted.]